THE ULTIMATE WORLD WAR I AND WORLD WAR II BOOK FOR KIDS

FASCINATING FACTS, BATTLES AND UNTOLD INSPIRING STORIES OF BRAVERY

DISCOVERING HISTORY IS FUN AND EASY

LION DIVINE

Copyright © 2022 by Lion Divine All rights reserved. This book or any portion thereof may not be reproduced or used in any manner whatsoever without the express written permission of the publisher except for the use of brief quotations in a book review.

For permission requests, write to the publisher, addressed "Attention: Permissions Coordinator," at the address below: loveliondivine @ gmail . com

Table of Contents

World War I	1
300 Incredible First World War Facts	6
The Brave Story of Sidney Lewis	47
The Heroic Story Albert Jacka	49
Jack Cornwall, The boy who never left his Post	52
Sergeant Alvin Cullum York	54
400 Amazing Second World War Facts	56
The story of Anne frank	107
Calvin graham: the 12-year-old navy hero	108
THE MOST FEARSOME SOLIDER OF WORLD WAR II: LIEUTENANT-COLONEL "MAD JACK" CHURCHILL	110
An American Hero: Charles Carpenter	112
The End	113

My Dear Friend

A thousand thanks for purchasing this book.
We really appreciate.
We are a small start-up publishing company and
thanks to you, we exist.
We are young, but we have big hearts and a big vision.

We do our best to offer the HIGHEST quality books for you to enjoy.
We are at the beginning of our journey, and nowadays, social proof is vital. Big corporations are coming with big budgets, and for them, it is easier to market their products. We are not yet able to compete with them.

If you enjoy this book, we have a very modest request: please take a few seconds to leave us a review on this book's Amazon product page

THE FIRST WORLD WAR

At the time, World War I was the largest and most awful war that had ever taken place. About 20 million people were killed, and 21 million people were injured. It was so bad that people called it "The War To End All Wars" because they believed people would never fight again. The people were hopeful, but wrong. Another war began just 21 years later. World War II was even more deadly than the first war. It took the lives of up to 60 million people.

World War I began in 1914 following the assassination of the Archduke Franz Ferdinand of Austria (pictured left). Ferdinand was the heir to the Austro-Hungarian Empire. The assassination of the Archduke and his wife triggered the war, but the reasons for the war are more complicated. A dreadful combination of imperialism and bad foreign policy created an atmosphere of animosity between nations for many years before any declarations of war were made.

The two main groups against each other were the Allies and the Central Powers. The Allies included Great Britain, France, Belgium, the United States, Italy, Russia, Japan, Montenegro, Serbia, Portugal, Romania, and Greece. The Central Powers were made up of Germany, Austria-Hungary, Bulgaria, and Turkey (the Ottoman Empire).

At the time, European and Middle Eastern dynasties were increasing their territories around the world. The British Empire, the German Empire, the Ottoman Empire, the Russian Empire, the Romanov Empire, and the Austro-Hungarian Empire were all involved in the First World War; citizens from countries ruled by one of these Empires went to war too, and many people from Asia and Africa fought in the war because of this.

World War I involved 135 countries, although most battles were in Europe and on the Western and Eastern Front.

The Americans didn't join the war at first. President Woodrow Wilson wanted to keep the peace until the Germans attacked and sunk a ship named the Lusitania in May 1915. One thousand one hundred ninety-five people were killed, 128 of whom were American citizens. Americans were no longer safe, and the military had to act.

By the winter of 1918, the Central Powers were losing the war; they could not keep fighting. On the 11th hour of the 11th day, of the 11th month, the First World War ended when both sides agreed to an Armistice. After this, both sides began peace talks.

In 1919 the Treaty of Versailles was signed by the Allies and the Germans; the Germans accepted guilt for the war and agreed to limit their army to just 100,000 men, pay the equivalent of $33 billion for the damage they caused in the war and give up all of their overseas territories and give land to the surrounding countries, they lost about 13% of Germany.

The German people were left humiliated following their defeat, and they were suffering because of the financial crisis after the war. In the 1930s, Adolf Hitler and the Nazi Party became popular with their ideas of restoring Germany to a wealthy and powerful nation.

The Nazis also blamed Jewish people for suffering in Germany. They believed Jewish people controlled the world, and the Nazis promised to fight against Jewish powers in Germany.

In 1933 he was elected Chancellor of Germany. He went on to pass laws that would allow him to rule as a dictator with complete control over the country.

Hitler started mobilizing and arming the German army, ignoring the Treaty of Versailles as he promised. In 1939 Germany invaded neighboring Poland. World War II has begun. Battle lines were drawn, and once again, two groups of nations were at war. The Allies included Great Britain, France, the United States, Poland, Canada, Norway, the Soviet Union, and more. While the Axis powers included Germany, Japan, and Italy.

This war was more ferocious and bloody than any other conflict. Tanks, fast planes, submarines, modern warships, and advanced weaponry made World War II a war of machines and metal.
The Germans used a new and effective method to invade countries. They called it Blitzkrieg, which means 'lightning war'. The Germans quickly attacked from the air and landed at the same time.

The Germans used these tactics successfully many times throughout the war. They took most of Europe and occupied it until the Allies regrouped and attacked the Germans on June 6th, 1944. The Allies used the same tactics as the Germans to take back Europe. The Allies pushed the Germans back, and on May 8th, 1945, the Germans surrendered. Peace had now returned to the world.

300 INCREDIBLE FIRST WORLD WAR FACTS

Explore one of the most interesting periods of human history with these amazing facts.

The war started for many political reasons, but one key trigger was the assassination of Archduke Franz Ferdinand and his pregnant wife Sophie, the Duchess of Hohenburg. A Serbian terrorist group known as the Black Hand shot the couple dead.

One reason for political trouble in Europe was the instability of the Balkans. The Balkans is a region in South-East Europe and includes countries such as Serbia, Montenegro, Kosovo, North Macedonia, and Romania. At the start of the 20th-century, war broke out in the region and it created tensions between Empires such as the Romanov Empire and the Austro-Hungarian Empire. They fought over land, and who should rule it.

The terrorist organization known as the Black Hand wanted to unite the Slavic people into one nation. Their motto was unification or death.

We have given the First World War many names. These names include The War To End All Wars, The Great War, Kaisers War, Kaiser Bills War, and World War I.

Before the First World War, the second most commonly spoken language in America was German, but they discouraged the use of the language when they went to war. They even stopped teaching German in schools.

Over 65 million men were involved in the war, this includes the soldiers from the Central Powers and the Allies. Some of these men were volunteers, but they conscripted many.

The world leaders at the time of the Great War included Nicholas II, he was the tsar of Russia. King George V was the king of England and Kaiser Wilhelm II, the German Emperor. Surprisingly, all three men are in the same family. In fact, they are all cousins. They all shared Queen Victoria as their grandmother, but they went to war with each other.

The terrorist organization known as the Black Hand wanted to unite the Slavic people into one nation. Their motto was unification or death.

We have given the First World War many names. These names include The War To End All Wars, The Great War, Kaisers War, Kaiser Bills War, and World War I.

Before the First World War, the second most commonly spoken language in America was German, but they discouraged the use of the language when they went to war. They even stopped teaching German in schools.

Over 65 million men were involved in the war, this includes the soldiers from the Central Powers and the Allies. Some of these men were volunteers, but they conscripted many.

The world leaders at the time of the Great War included Nicholas II, he was the tsar of Russia. King George V was the king of England and Kaiser Wilhelm II, the German Emperor. Surprisingly, all three men are in the same family. In fact, they are all cousins. They all shared Queen Victoria as their grandmother, but they went to war with each other.

About 30 countries were involved in World War I.

The youngest person to fight in the Great War was Sidney Lewis, he was 12 years old. He lied about his age to join the British army.

The oldest British man to fight was 71 years old and his name was Robert Frederick Robertson.

16,000 British men refused to fight. These are called conscientious objectors. They sent some to prison and others did menial jobs, like pig farming.

Americans were not punished for not wanting to fight, instead, they were given non-combative jobs, like cooks and drivers.

Clergymen (priests, vicars, and pastors) did not have to go to war, nor did teachers. Everyone else between the ages of 18 and 41 had to fight (unless disabled).

They did not punish Americans for being conscientious objectors. Instead, they were given non-combative roles to help with the war effort.

The Great War began on July 28th, 1914, when Austria-Hungary made a declaration of war against Serbia. France, Russia, and Great Britain all joined the war in the following week.

Russia had the biggest army, with over 5 million troops.

Britain had less than 1 million soldiers, but soon they would grow the army to have over 3 million troops.

27% of all Scottish men over the age of 15 joined the war by 1915.

Belgium and America remained neutral at the start of the war.

When the war first started, everyone thought it would be finished by Christmas, less than six months away.

The fast German battle plan is called the Schlieffen Plan.

The Schlieffen Plan required the German forces to invade and take over France in 6 weeks or fewer.

The Germans mobilized a total of 1.5 million men alongside the French and Belgian borders.

The Central Powers also sent men to the east to attack Russia. The double invasion, one to the east and one to the west, created the two fronts.

The western front and the eastern front are the two main areas where fighting between both powers took place.

The first battle took place in the heavily defended city of Liege in Belgium, on August 5th, 1914, even though the Belgians were a neutral nation.

The city of Liege is built alongside the river Meuse and is built on top of a 500-foot slope, making it difficult to attack.

12 heavily armed forts defended the city. At the time, they considered Liege to be an impenetrable city.

The German Field Marshall Karl von Bulow felt confident his 320,000 troops would easily defeat the 35,000 Belgian troops guarding the city, but he meet unexpected resistance from the Belgians. They fought for days. Eventually, the Germans used their strongest weaponry to take the city of Liege.

To capture the city of Liege, the Germans used the largest cannons ever built. On August 12th, the Germans used their heavy artillery to destroy the walls of the forts and by the 15th they had taken the city and captured the Belgian general.

After the Germans took Liege, they continued to pass through Belgium towards France, destroying all the towns they encountered and killing civilians.

The German Field Marshall Karl von Bulow felt confident his 320,000 troops would easily defeat the 35,000 Belgian troops guarding the city, but he meet unexpected resistance from the Belgians. They fought for days. Eventually, the Germans used their strongest weaponry to take the city of Liege.

To capture the city of Liege, the Germans used the largest cannons ever built. On August 12th, the Germans used their heavy artillery to destroy the walls of the forts and by the 15th they had taken the city and captured the Belgian general.

After the Germans took Liege, they continued to pass through Belgium towards France, destroying all the towns they encountered and killing civilians.

On September 6th, 1914, the French and British armies fought the German army in the First Battle of the Marne. The fight took place in the North East of France, less than 40 miles from the French capital, Paris.

The Allies successfully pushed the Germans back. The First Battle of Marne lasted for 3 days and the plan to quickly take France had failed. The Allies had created a strong defense and fought bravely against the Central Powers.

In the fall of 1914, the Central Powers and Allies dug trenches along the western front. Everyone got settled down for a longer war than expected.

The battlegrounds to the east of Germany are called the Eastern Front. The area to the west of Germany is the Western Front.

In the summer of 1914, Russian soldiers quickly took German and Austro-Hungarian land to the east. To fight against the invading Russian forces, the Central powers moved soldiers from the west to come and fight in the east against the Russians.

The German and Austrian armies were able to stop the progress of the Russians when they were victorious at the Battle of Tannenberg in August 1914.

166,000 German soldiers fought in the Battle of Tannenberg and around 206,000 Russian soldiers. About 50,000 Russians died during the battle and 13,000 German soldiers died.

A further 92,000 Russian soldiers were taken prisoner by the German forces.

On Christmas day 1914, German and Allied troops came out of the trenches and played a game of football with each other. They sang Christmas carols too.

In late 1914, the Ottoman Empire entered the war on the side of the Central Powers. A new battleground in the Middle East opened up.

The Allies wanted to invade the Ottoman Empire and take the city of Constantinople. The British Navy (and some French soldiers) sent ships and troops to the Gallipoli Peninsula (modern-day Turkey) on the coast of the Aegean Sea.

On November 3rd, 1914, the British began firing at Turkish forts alongside a narrow channel called the Dardanelles.

In February 1915 Allied marines step onto the shores of Turkey and meet little resistance from the Ottomans, but in March the Ottomans sunk three battleships with heavy artillery fire from the land. The Navy withdrew and requested support from the army.

In April 1915, the Allies (French, New Zealand, and Australia), led by the British, invaded Gallipoli in force. Some groups were able to secure beaches, but with great difficulty. The Allies could not progress through the land.

By September 1915, it was clear that the Allies could not take the Peninsula or Constantinople. They ended the assault. All troops were withdrawn by January 1916.

Gallipoli is seen as a military failure by the Allies, although the fighting helped the Russians because it distracted the Ottoman forces.

Over 200,000 British soldiers were killed in total. This was a disaster for the Allies.

Winston Churchill (who will become Prime Minister of Britain), was the First Lord of the British Admiralty, he oversaw the disastrous Gallipoli operations. Churchill felt great shame and guilt for his role in the death of so many British men. He resigned his command, and the Navy demoted him. He joined the army and served as an officer for the rest of the war.

The Battle of the Somme is one of the most famous and deadly battles to take place on the Western Front. It started in July 1916 and ended in November 1916.

It began as the Allies tried to attack the German defenses, but it was unsuccessful.

On the first day, 57,000 British troops died. Making it the deadliest day in British military history.

In the end, over 3 million soldiers died, and many were injured too.

The first American was killed in the Battle of the Somme before the United States joined the war. Harry Butters was serving with the British army and he was killed on the 31st of August 1916.

The Allied troops fired over 1.7 million artillery shells at German defenses during the Battle of the Somme.

The heavy firing was supposed to destroy the German barbed wire and allow men to get through, but it failed to do so. The barbed wire remained intact in many places and prevented the soldiers from easily attacking the Germans.

The Battle of Somme is the first battle in history to use a tank. 48 Mark One tanks were deployed by the British. Unfortunately, they were not very reliable and most of them broke down,

In 141 days of continuous fighting, the Allies only advanced 7 miles and never broke the German front line.

In 1917, the Russian people had a revolution. They were angry and upset about food shortages, battle losses, and economic instability. Vladimir Lenin and the Bolsheviks led the revolution. They imprisoned the Russian Czar Nicholas II and his family, and he abdicated his throne. From this point on, the Russians were no longer involved in the war and Russia would be changed forever.

The Battle of Caporetto took place in Italy. The German and Austro-Hungarian forces pushed the Italians back, and they were victorious.

The Allies sent support to the Italians and helped them take back Italy from the Central Powers.

If the enemy captures a soldier alive, they would become prisoners of war, which are commonly called POWs. For the duration of the war, these men are sent to prison.

At the end of the war, they release POWs.

At the start of the war, the Americans didn't want to fight. They tried to keep peace with the Allies and the Central Powers.

Some American citizens joined the war on behalf of other nations. Many of them went to the French Foreign Legion, others drove ambulances.

The Germans used their U-boats (submarines) to attack ships in the Atlantic Ocean. They sunk many passenger and cargo ships, even some American ships.

Although the United States was officially neutral. President Woodrow publically condemned the Germans for sinking British and French ships but did not condemn the British blockade of German ships. This showed the president's true feelings and allegiances before the Americans ever joined the war.

President Woodrow Wilson allowed American banks to make very large loans to the Allies to support the war effort against the Central Powers.

In May 1915, the Lusitania was sunk with over 100 US citizens onboard. This angered Americans back home, as the public wanted to go to war against the Germans. The constant sinking of American ships changed the mind of the American president.

On April 2nd, 1917, the American president Woodrow Wilson went before the US Congress and formerly asked them to make a declaration of war. America had now joined the Allies against the Central Powers. They sent ships and men across the ocean to Europe.

There were rumors that the Mexicans were planning on making allegiance with the Germans. A Telegram from the Germans and Mexicans was intercepted, and it proposed that the Mexicans and Germans work together and the Germans would help the Mexicans get lost territories back from the Americans. Texas, Arizona, and New Mexico were all lost by Mexico in the Mexican-American war. This is another reason the Americans entered the war.

BY 1918, OVER 10,000 AMERICAN SOLDIERS WERE LANDING IN FRANCE EVERY SINGLE DAY. THIS BOOSTED THE MORALE OF THE ALLIED TROOPS A LOT. IT THRILLED THEM TO SEE FRESH AND HEALTHY AMERICAN SOLDIERS AFTER YEARS OF WAR.

OVERALL, THE AMERICANS SENT OVER 2 MILLION TROOPS TO EUROPE TO FIGHT ALONGSIDE THE ALLIES. OVER 50,000 AMERICANS DIED DURING THE CONFLICT.

13,000 Native Americans fought in the war, even though they were not formally recognized as U.S citizens at the time.

Native Americans from the Choctaw tribe helped the Americans by translating messages into their language and then sending these messages to the Allies, the Germans were unable to translate them and the messages stay secret. There was no word for a machine gun in the Choctaw language so they called machine guns 'little gun shoot fast'.

Over 200,000 African Americans went to war, but they were segregated.

A famous African American unit was named the Harlem Hell Fighters and the men who fought in this military unit were given the Croix de Guerre (a French medal) for their bravery.

Despite the bravery of the African American community, their good deeds were mostly ignored back home.

The war did help improve the lives of African Americans; Henry Ford employed some to work in his factories.

The United States was involved in 13 campaigns in World War I. These campaigns include The Battle of Cambrai, the Battle of Lys, Cantigny, and the Somme Defensive.

American military engineers were sent to help the British because they had lost many of the engineers in the war and needed help on the last day of the Battle of Cambrai. Sadly, some of these engineers were the first American soldiers to die in World War I.

The Battle of Argonne Forest was one of the most deadly battles for the Americans. In total, 117,000 men were killed or wounded during the campaign.

The American soldiers who came to Europe were called the AEF, which means the American Expeditionary Forces. These are for troops who go abroad.

Walt Disney volunteered to be an ambulance driver in the war.

The Americans needed more money to pay for the war. They raised taxes to get this money from the American people.

The Americans joined the war in April 1917 and were involved until the end.

The Americans sent 70,000 horses and donkeys to Europe to help with the war effort.

Hello, Girls is the name given to the American women who worked for the American Telephone and Telegraph Company. They spoke French and English.

During the war, 223 women served as Hello Girls, they were sent to France, and some were stationed in a range of German artillery. None died in combat, although two of the women died from the Spanish Flu.

At first, the military enlisted men to work as call operators, but they weren't very good at the job. It took a man about 60 seconds to connect a call, whereas women took about 10 seconds.

The Hello Girls were not acknowledged for their important role during the war until the 1970s. By which time, many had already died.
Over 7 million pro-war speeches were made in America; these speeches took place in movie theaters and other public venues.

Frankfurter sausages were renamed liberty sausages by the American people because Frankfurt is a German city.

Hamburgers were renamed Salisbury steak because of their association with the German city of Hamburg.

American citizens of German heritage were treated badly during the war. One American German was killed during anti-German protests.

After World War 1 had finished, America had created the world's largest military.

The Allies had a superior Navy to the Central Powers. Britain had better quality ships and more ships than the Germans, but the Germans had U-Boats. U-Boats are underwater submarines that are armed with torpedos; they can sink ships without anyone even knowing they are there.

The conflict between the Central Powers and the Allies occurred in every ocean on the planet.

The Germans were highly successful at sinking ships with their submarines. At one point, Britain only had a few weeks' supplies of grain before they would run out and the people would go hungry and starve. This is because the Germans were sinking a quarter of all British supply ships.

About 6,000 Allied ships were sunk by German U-boats.

In 1915, the British Navy launched a surprise attack on the German fleet in a battle known as the Battle of Dogger Bank in the North Sea. The British were superior and won the encounter.

Five Allied warships and 4 German ships were involved in the battle. The Allied ships were the Lion, the Tiger, Princess Royal, New Zealand, and the Indomitable. The four German ships were the Seydlitz, Moltke, Derfflinger and Blucher.

The Tiger, the Lion, and Indomitable were all torpedoed by the Germans, but Princess Royal and New Zealand were unhit. They hit all the German ships except the Moltke.

The Blucher was sunk, and the Seydlitz was badly damaged. One hundred fifty-nine people were killed on the Seydlitz, and they killed 729 sailors when the Blucher sank.

The biggest naval battle of the First World War was the Battle of Jutland. It took place in May 1916. Once again, the British were the superior naval force. After the Battle of Jutland, the Germans never tried to fight the Allies at sea again.

The British used a naval blockade to stop food and supplies from getting to Germany on the sea. They did this to force Germany to surrender and end the war.

Olympic, the sister ship to the famous Titanic, was the only civilian ship to sink a U-boat. They did this by ramming the U-boat with the side of the ship.

German contact mines sank many Allied warships. These mines were the most effective weapon the Germans had against the Allied Navy.

Although the First World War was mechanized, both the Allies and the Central Powers still relied heavily on animals for many jobs.

They used elephants in World War I to carry loads and plow fields. The elephants used were from Lord Sangers Circus, so they were already trained to follow commands.

Pigeons were used to carry messages between the frontline and command. The Germans used birds of prey for hunting and killing the pigeons.

A particular pigeon named Cher Ami saved the lives of over 500 American soldiers when she transported messages of distress to command. She lost an eye and a leg, but the army vets worked hard to save her life and made a wooden leg. They awarded her a medal for bravery, named the Croix de Guerre.

Horses were used in the war too, and they were used for general transportation and warfare. They even carried wounded soldiers away from the battlefield to the field hospitals.

Soldiers on horseback are called the Cavalry.

About 8 million horses were killed in the Great War.

A baboon named Jackie was bought to the western front by South African soldiers. She was used to warning the troops of enemy movement. If she heard something, she would alarm the troops by shouting or tugging on soldiers' clothing.

Some soldiers kept animals as pets or mascots. The HMS Irresistible had a cat named Togo, while the RAF had a fox as their mascot.

Soldiers kept chickens in the trenches so they could collect the eggs to supplement their rations.

A famous donkey named Jimmy, the sergeant was born during the Battle of the Somme; he was injured multiple times during the war but still learned how to salute with his front leg.

Dogs were given messengers to send from the front line to command. They were better suited to sending messages than humans because they were smaller and could easily sneak past enemies.

They used dogs to find injured soldiers on the battlefield, too. Their strong sense of smell makes them ideal for sniffing out bleeding soldiers.

Dogs could also detect poisonous gases before humans noticed them. They were trained to bark when they smelled gas.

About 1 million dogs died during the war.

Scientists discovered that slugs could detect gases before humans. When deadly gases were present, slugs close their breathing pores and compress their bodies. They gave soldiers slugs to keep as gas warnings. They called these slugs the 'slug brigade'.

During the First World War, the American military created the veterinary corps to tend to the health and injuries of the animals. They employed veterinary surgeons, nurses, and stable hands.

A trench is a long, and deep ditch dug into the ground by soldiers. Normally, they are about 3 meters deep and 1 to 2 meters wide. They were laid out in a zig-zag pattern, not straight lines.

Trench warfare is the term used to describe the type of fighting that commonly occurred during World War I. men fight over inches of land from their trenches.

Both the Allies and the Central Powers dug trenches along the western front. These trenches stretched from the coast of Belgium to the mountains in Switzerland. In total, there were about 475 miles of trenches across Europe.

The trenches protected the soldiers from being shot or gassed.

The area between the trenches of the Allies and the Central Powers is called 'no-man's-land'. This is a very dangerous place. They covered it with barbed wire and machine guns and heavy artillery from both sides were constantly watching it and firing upon it.

The trenches on the western front were built by 90,000 Chinese laborers which were brought in to help with the war effort.

The trenches were a cramped and dirty place to be. Often they were very muddy and boggy too. These unsanitary conditions caused the disease to spread quickly. Cholera, influenza, and dysentery were all common in the trenches.

Most soldiers spent four days at a time in the frontline trenches.

Trench foot is a disease caused by living in wet and dirty trench conditions. Trench foot causes the skin on foot to die. In severe cases, men had to have their feet amputated.

Trench mouth is a painful disease common in the men who lived in the trenches, it caused the mouth and gums to be infected and inflamed.

Rats and other vermin lived in the trenches of the First World War too. They were a big problem for the men who lived in the trenches. The rats would steal food from the soldiers while they were sleeping. They stole so much food that the rats became huge. Some said they were the same size as a domestic cat.

Rats spread disease because they spread their disease-ridden feces and urine as they move around.

The rats were a problem for most World War I soldiers, but for some, they were a comfort. They enjoyed their company and even kept their favorite rat as a pet.

Some soldiers were less comforted by the presence of the rats. They used cats and small dogs called Terriers to keep them away.

Other pests in the trenches include lice and mosquitos. They spread disease too, including the deadly disease Malaria, which is carried by mosquitos.

The lice in the trenches spread a disease called trench fever. It caused headaches, fever, and pain. It made the men sick for 3 months.

Sleeping in the trenches was difficult, but to give the men a small amount of peace, they would dig underground shelters or shallow hollows to sleep in.

Going to the toilet in the trenches was a challenge. They had no plumbing. Everyone had to use pits. These pits were about 5 feet deep, and the men called them latrines.

Because of the lack of plumbing, the trenches were very dirty and smelly. This unclean environment helped to spread deadly diseases and viruses.

The trenches were so dirty and disease-ridden that every two weeks, the men had to be taken away from the front line to b thoroughly cleaned, given new clothing, and deloused (this means receiving lice treatment).

They constructed trenches with sandbags, barbed wire, and wooden planks. Although some are just made with mud.

The trenches were often flooded. It was common for soldiers to be knee-deep in muddy water. This is one of the reasons soldiers had trench foot.

As the war progressed, the trenches became cluttered with broken or unwanted items. Wooden boxes, empty cartridges, and torn uniforms littered the narrow space.

Periscope

Although the trenches protected soldiers most of the time, sometimes trenches made things more dangerous. Soldiers could get trapped in the trench and have nowhere to escape from enemy fire.

Soldiers used a periscope to look out the top of trenches without risking being shot.

The men enjoyed listening to music while they were in the trenches, it helped to take their minds away from the hard times they were facing.

When soldiers were away from the front line, they could spend time in Salvation Army huts and tents. Different nations set up these large huts to provide the men with somewhere comfortable to eat, write letters, socialize and relax.

There were over 180 huts set up during the war. Some of these huts would have over 5,000 men visit in a day.

Soldiers often had instruments. Popular instruments in the trenches included harmonicas, violins, cellos, guitars, and trumpets.

Lots of different songs were played in the First World War. Some of the most popular tunes of the time were 'It's a long way to Tipperary' and 'pack up your troubles in your old kitbag'.

The Allies and the Central Powers all dug tunnels underneath no-man's-land. Their goal was to plant explosives and destroy enemy trenches.

They brought professional miners from Great Britain to the Western Front to dig these tunnels.

In 1917, during the Battle of Messines, they distributed 455 tons of explosives through over 20 tunnels, which took a year to plan and build. The plan resulted in a giant explosion which took the lives of Over 10,000 Germans.
The huge explosion on the German front lines was so loud that they could hear it in England, over 140 miles away.

World War I saw significant changes and developments in weaponry. Many of the weapons used were used for the first time in the history of warfare.

Depth charges (also known as depth bombs) are canisters filled with explosive materials. They were rolled off the back of battleships into the area they expected German submarines to be lurking. They were first used in the First World War. Most of the time, the depth charge exploded too far away from the submarine to destroy it, but it would damage the submarine enough to force it to the surface where the navy could capture or destroy it.

Rifles were commonly given to infantry soldiers. They were significantly more advanced than the weapons used just a few decades before the war.

Commonly used rifles include the Lee-Enfield. 303 rifle (used by the British) and the Springfield 306 (used by the Americans).

American officers designed the Mark One Trench Knife and issued to soldiers in 1918. It was designed to be used for close-quarter fighting in the trenches. It has a double-edged dagger blade.

Battleships were used heavily during the war. The strength of the British navy helped the Allies defeat the German U-boats.

Due to shortages in steel, they made some battleships from concrete.

Submarines were made famous by the German U-boats, but the Allies developed them eight years before the war.

They equipped submarines with torpedo guns that could be used under the water without altering the enemy to the presence of the submarine, or they could fire a machine gun above the water.

The Germans built over 300 submarines.

The Germans sunk half of all British cargo ships.

Artillery was a key component of warfare. Both sides of the war used them on all fronts.

Artillery weapons used in the Great war include the 420mm, Big Bertha.

Artillery was responsible for more deaths than any other weapon type.

The German soldiers called the French artillery weapons 'devil guns'.

Mortar weapons are similar to artillery pieces. The main difference between the two weapons is mortars are normally smaller and fire their ammunition in a vertical direction, but an artillery piece sends its rounds horizontally.

The mortar was developed in 1915 by the British, and their role was to damage enemy trenches.

Mortar weapons could fire 22 shells per minute, with a range of about 1,200 yards.

The German version of a mortar was called the minenwerfer (mine thrower), and it fired metal balls.

All nations used machine guns, most machine guns used were based on the Hiram Maxim 1884, a weapon that can fire up to 600 rounds per minute.

Tanks were first used during the Frist World War, although they were only used in supporting roles because they were unreliable. The idea for tanks dates back to medieval times, when Leonardo da Vinci, the great inventor and artist, made detailed drawings of 'land battleships.

Tanks were all assigned a gender. A male tank had a canon, while female tanks had machine guns.

The first British-made tank was known as 'Little Willie', and its max speed was 3 miles per hour, and it weighed over 14 tons.

Tanks were so unreliable because they regularly broke down on the battlefield that the commanders of the First World War believed they would never be used significantly in any future war.

Flamethrowers were used, especially by Germans. The German flamethrower could produce flames 20 yards away.

The Germans used the first flamethrower in 1915 near Verdun.

During the entire First World War, the Germans launched over 650 flamethrower attacks on the Allies and used over 3000 flamethrower troops.

A flamethrower troop carried a tank on his back, like a backpack. Inside the tank was pressurized fuel. Which was lit on fire as it left through a handheld nozzle.

The Allies developed their flamethrower technology but used them a lot less than the Germans did.

Chemical weapons were deployed widely during the war. Chemical weapons are gases and chemicals which are released purposefully to hurt the enemy soldiers when they breathe them in.

They added the chemicals to artillery shells, cylinders, and grenade cartridges.

About 30 different types of deadly gases were used during the war.

They used three main types of chemical weapons during the First World War, these are mustard gas, chlorine gas, and phosgene.

Mustard gas causes blisters on the skin. Some say it smells of gasoline; others say garlic and dead horses. Most of the time, when deployed in battle, the concentrations in the air weren't strong enough to kill people immediately. A few hours after exposure, soldiers would go blind and experience severe eye pain. When the blisters would pop, they often became infected. Mustard gas killed approximately 120,000 people during the war.

Chlorine gas is greeny-yellow color. It smells like bleach. When soldiers came into contact with it, their breathing is badly affected and when the gas is in a high enough concentration, it can cause near-immediate death.

Phosgene is like chlorine gas but much stronger. It's also invisible and smells like hay. It would take a few days for the victim to die, their lungs would fill with water and they would die a very painful death

The French were the first to use chemical weapons in World War I, they used tear gas grenades, and in the end, most nations used them.

Phosgene was responsible for 85% of all chemical weapon deaths, making it super deadly.

By the end of the war, chemical weapons had killed 1.3 million people.

The Germans tried to attack the Russians with chemical weapons, but the extremely cold temperatures stopped the chemicals from vaporizing and affecting the troops' health.

10% of all American Artillery shells had some form of chemical weapon inside.

Troops used a urine-soaked cloth to try and stop the effect of the deadly gases.

In 1918 effective gas masks were introduced to the military.

A trench raiding club was a homemade weapon made by both the Allies and the Central Powers. It often included a bat or a thick wooden stick that would have barbed wire added to it. They would use them against the enemy in quiet nighttime raids of the enemy trenches.

British soldiers only used helmets in 1915. Until this point, they used cloth hats.

Helmets were not bulletproof, although they offered some protection against shrapnel.

World War I was the first war where more soldiers died in combat than from disease.

Donkeys and horses were used as ambulances to carry wounded soldiers to doctors at the start of the war, but after injured soldiers were left in the rain with no help, the idea for motorized ambulances was born.

Countless medical improvements were created by the doctors tending to the injured soldiers.

At the start of the war, the main role of doctors was to amputate injured limbs, but as time and advancements progressed, they were able to prevent many amputations with the new techniques they had developed.

The main reason for amputations during the Great War was an infection, not because of the seriousness of the initial injury; about 70% of amputations were caused by infection.

The chances of a soldier surviving an amputation had massively increased by the Great War; only about 5% of soldiers who received amputations died, whereas in the Civil War, about 25% of amputations resulted in death.

The main cause of infection in wounded soldiers was trench conditions. If the men were injured whilst fighting from the trenches, they would be exposed to huge amounts of bacteria (because of the poor sanitary conditions).

Soldiers were regularly given a vaccination for tetanus.

As the war continued, wound care improved, the importance of disinfecting cuts became widely known by doctors and nurses, and the use of antiseptics such as Dakin's solution saved millions of lives.
For the first time, injuries to the abdomen and bowels could be routinely treated successfully by surgeons.

Radiography (X-rays) was used for the first time during a war. The technology was invented about 16 years earlier.

X-ray equipment was transported to battlefield hospitals so doctors could investigate injured soldiers' bones and take better care of them.

Blood transfusions and intravenous fluids were available for the first time.

Antibiotics were not available during the war.

At the same time as the Great War, the world was also experiencing a global influenza pandemic, commonly known as the Spanish Flu. The pandemic began in 1918, near the end of the war, and went on to kill about 50 million people, making it more deadly than the war.

Unlike earlier wars, anesthesia was now available, allowing surgeons to easily operate on 'sleeping' patients.

At the start of the war, there were just 491 American army doctors. By the end of the war, there were over 30,000 and 20,000 nurses.

The military also gave soldiers dental care. The Americans grow the number of dentists they had from just 86 to over 5,000.

During the First World War, they formed the Veterinary Corps. They took care of the millions of military animals. They also had to inspect meat and eggs and make sure it was fit for eating.

American Congress issued $30 million to be used for medical supplies and equipment.

57,000 American troops died from disease during the conflict.

A common disease that killed troops included measles, mumps, and gastroenteritis.

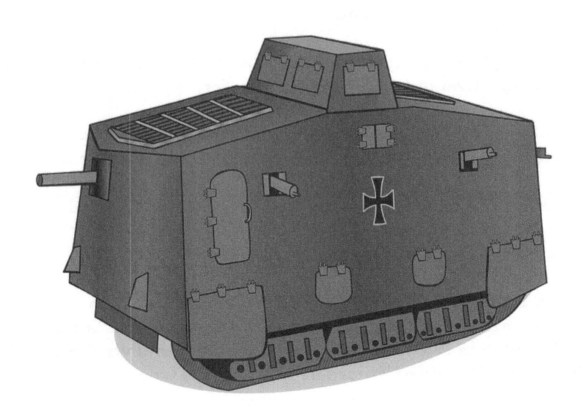

The Europeans had a serious shortage of medical professionals. When the Americans joined the war effort, they helped the Allies by sending American medical staff to work alongside the Europeans.

A charity known as the Red Cross helped the Allies in the war. They supported them with medical care and supplies.

Mental health services were not very good, many men suffered from shell shock, which is now known as Post Traumatic Stress Disorder. Men who were struggling emotionally were given a few days off and then sent back to war.

For the first time in the history of war, there was now a focus on rehabilitation for seriously injured troops. Special convalescent hospitals were used to help amputees learn how to walk again and manage other disabilities.

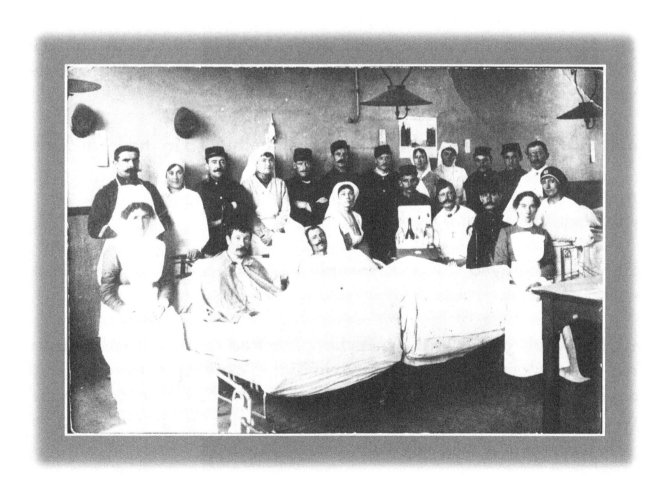

Facial injuries were common. Many men suffered from severe deformations in the face. This prompted advancements in plastic surgery to help these men eat, drink, speak, and feel better about their appearance.

A doctor from New Zealand named Dr. Harold Gillies pioneered research in plastic surgery; for the first time, faces could be reconstructed after serious injury, men arrived at Dr. Gillies's hospital ward in England without chins and eyes, but they left looking considerably better thanks to the new techniques.

Due to the emotional effect of men seeing the injuries to their faces, they banned mirrors in plastic surgery wards.

Doctors used artists and sculptors to create drawings of what the men looked like before they were injured to help the doctors build their faces back.

Another legendary doctor from the war is American citizen Varaztad Kazanjian. He came to America when he was a child and studied dentistry at Harvard Medical School. Varaztad went to France to help the soldiers there. He treated over 3,000 men and did such a good job that they called him the 'miracle man'; in the following years, the King of England, George V, honored him for his extraordinary work.

If soldiers died in hospital, they would then be buried in the local cemetery.

Men were well fed during the war; they were given up to 4,000 calories per day to keep them fit and healthy.

The British employed 300,000 people to make and distribute food to the troops.

They drank lots of tea in the trenches. The Red Cross helped distribute hot drinks to the men. They gave approximately 12 million cups of tea out. Other popular hot drinks given to the men include coffee and cocoa. These warm drinks were especially important when they were fighting in cold places.

The American and Australian troops preferred to drink coffee.

Men in the trenches could cook their hot food using a portable stove known as a Tommy Cooker.

The men had lots of tinned meats. One type of tinned meat is known as bully beef and was often disliked by the troops.

They were supplied with fresh vegetables such as carrots, turnips, and potatoes. They also had lots of biscuits and sweet cakes.

Men had emergency rations in case they could not get more food. These emergency rations included beef sugar biscuits and tea. The men were forbidden from opening these rations without direct orders from an officer or in serious emergencies.

They sent a huge amount of food from Britain to the front line, a total of 3,240,948 tons of food went to the western front for all the troops.

German Food Container

At the start of the war, rations for soldiers were larger. They gave men 10 ounces of meat and 8 ounces of vegetables, but because of supply problems, this had to be reduced.

Maconochie was one of the most common meals given to the men. It is a stew made from tinned beef with gravy and vegetables, it wasn't very nice, one soldier said "cold it is a man killer". Although it was technically made from beef, it contained mostly fat and gristle.

Because flour and wheat supplies were so low, the army had to make bread from ground turnips.

A type of bread known as K-Brot was made in the war years. It was made with anything that could be found, even straw on some occasions.

Even when they did have real bread, it was almost always stale because it took over a week for food to get to the front.

Due to the staleness of the bread and biscuits, the men broke them up and cooked them with vegetables and meat, just to make them edible.

When normal meat and vegetables were in short supply, cooks had to be resourceful to feed the men. They used nettles and horsemeat to substitute beef and vegetables.

The frontline soldiers often complained that officers were given more and better food.

Family members of the troops often sent food parcels to the frontline with treats like chocolate.

On Christmas Day, the people away from the frontline would have some form of a Christmas dinner. They would often find turkeys locally, but for the men on the front line, it was no different. They had all their usual rations unless their family sent something special.

They sometimes gave alcohol to the men in their rations. Beer and cider were the most common drinks.

The Home Front is a term used to describe the people living in Britain during the war.

In 1918, the British government introduced food rationing; milk, sugar, meat, flour, and butter were all controlled to prevent shortages.

When the war first broke out in Europe, people all over the continent held big parties in the street to celebrate; they believed the war would be quickly won.

Governments involved in the war created propaganda to convince the population to help with the war in any way they could.

The men who did not go to war were shunned by society; they were often refused service in shops. They were given white feathers, making them easily identifiable.

The British government tried to hide the horrors of the war from the people. They didn't want to reduce morale in the country, so they brought injured soldiers back into London at night.

The expense of the war hit the people at home badly, food and fuel prices rose, and it made life difficult for people, especially poor people.

There were lots of shortages; this was caused by the German U-boats sinking cargo ships, which meant people had to be resourceful to get by.

To help substitute the food shortages, citizens of Allied countries were encouraged by the government to grow lots of fruits and vegetables. They called these victory gardens. These victory gardens were planted in the private gardens of citizens and public gardens.

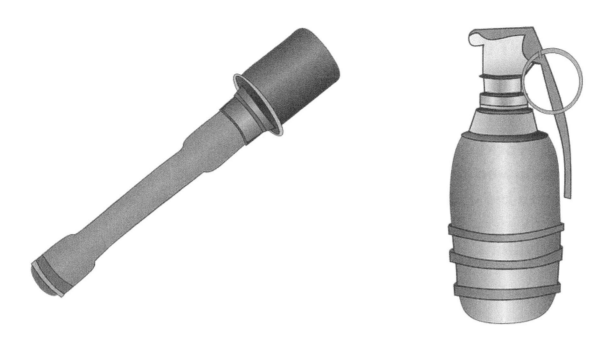

They introduced rationing in 1918 in Britain to make sure that everyone got enough food.

Rationing was never introduced in America. Instead, the government asked the people to be responsible and consider the needs of the military.

Up until war broke out, men had been the people who ran the factories and worked in them, but now with so many men away at war, they needed women to help, especially to produce weapons. For the first time in history, women were doing work that only men had done.

Although women were very important to the war effort, and without them, there would not have been enough men to do all vital jobs, many were not happy about women doing 'men's work'. They worried about whether women would be capable of doing the work and what would happen to the men when they returned from war.

The women who worked in munition factories were called Munitionettes or Canary Girls.

During the war, almost 1 million women worked in munitions factories.

Some men were not happy about women working and wearing trousers.

It was common for factory workers' skin to turn yellow because of damage caused by the TNT they were handling.

The munitions factories had to work 24/7 to meet the military's demand.

Women were working so hard in the factories that safety procedures were not always followed to save time. This meant sometimes terrible accidents happened, even big explosions and fires in which people died.

1500 British civilians were killed during the war because of factory-related accidents.

Women proved they could work just as well as men during the war and went on to get equal rights over the next century.

American women were given the right to vote in 1919.

Most British women were given the right to vote in 1918.

Allied nations suffered financially when the war ended; they all had lots of debts and high levels of unemployment.

Britain lost its position as the world superpower after the end of the war.

After the war ended and the surviving men returned, the people had many children; the time that followed is known as the baby boom.

Almost 1 million men from the British Empire were killed.

Australians were killed more than any other group of men from the British Empire; about 65% of all Australian troops were killed or injured.

The end of World War 1 saw the end of four historical empires, the Ottoman Empire, the German Empire, the Romanov Empire, and the Austro-Hungarian Empire were all finished.

The Russian royal family was all killed by the Bolsheviks, and the country became the first communist nation in the world.

After the First World War, Finland, Lithuania, Latvia, Estonia, and Poland were all formed into independent countries.

At the end of the war, France took control of Syria.

Germany was economically destroyed by the end of the war and the Treaty of Versailles, they were forced to pay billions of dollars, and the German people experienced great poverty.

Many Germans were angry with their leaders for signing the treaty and did not accept that they had lost the war. They called the men who signed the treaty on Germany's behalf 'November Criminals'.

In total, five treaties were signed between the Allies and the Central Powers, although the Treaty of Versailles was the most punishing and famous.

Some people predicted that there would be another war; the French general Ferdinand Foch said, "This is not peace; this is an Armistice for twenty years," and he was correct.

The poppy flower has represented the Great War. Many modern-day organizations and charities use the poppy to represent servicemen and women, and veterans.

This iconic poppy symbol was made because of a famous poem by Lieutenant Colonel John McCrae M.D. He wrote:

> In Flanders Fields, the poppies blow
> Between the crosses, row on row,
> That mark our place; and in the sky
> The larks, still bravely singaing, fly
> Scarce heard amid the guns below.
>
> We are the Dead. Short days ago
> We lived, felt dawn, saw sunset glow,
> Loved and were loved, and now we lie
> In Flanders fields.
>
> Take up our quarrel with the foe:
> To you, from failing hands, we throw
> The torch; be yours to hold it high.
> If ye break faith with us who die
> We shall not sleep, though poppies grow
> In Flanders fields.

On the 11th of November, people worldwide celebrate Armistice Day, which is the day the war ended.

Many of the trenches have been left in Europe as a memorial to the men who died there, and people can go and visit them.

On Armistice Day, people lay wreaths at war memorials and hold a minute's silence to remember those who have died in the war.

The Brave Story of Sidney Lewis

This is the story of perhaps the bravest 12-year-old boy ever to live. When war broke out in Europe, London boy Sidney was too young to fight; at just 12 years old, he would have to wait another four years until he was 16 and older enough to legally join the war and fight for his country.

For most young boys, that would be the end of their dream to serve their country, but Sidney didn't let it stop him. He created a plan to make sure he did his part in the Great War. One day he ran away from his family home; his parents had no idea that young Sidney was on his way to the army recruitment office.
The recruitment officers asked him his age, and he lied, he told them he was 18, and somehow, they believed him and accepted him into the military.

Following some basic training, Sidney was sent to the heart of the war; he was on the front line in France. Sidney would go on to be a part of the worst battle in British military history, the Battle of the Somme, where 125,000 British troops died. The fighting was so horrendous that all the trees in the woodland were turned into blackened stumps, except for just one tree. By some miracle, Sidney managed to survive the bloody battle.

Back home, Sidney's mother was worried sick about her young son. She read horror stories in the newspaper about the terrible battles taking place. She wasn't at all happy about him being there so she decided to do something about it and try to get him home. She wrote to the War Office and sent Sidney's birth certificate, which proved the boy's true age. His mother demanded he immediately is returned to England.

The British high command worked to rescue Sidney at the request of his mother, but they were fearful they would be too late, and he would die before they got to him. Luckily their messengers managed to find Sidney after he had been fighting for over 6 weeks in France and been away from home for almost a year.

They pulled Sidney back from the front line and sent him home to London, where his mother was relieved to see him once again. He went on to live a full and long life; he got married and had a family of his own. His son didn't believe that his father went to France because of his young age at the time of the war, but now they know the truth and are all very proud of him and how brave he was.

The Heroic Story Albert Jacka

Albert Jacka was born on a small farm in Australia in 1893; he was one of seven children. His friends and family called him Burt, and he was fairly short, measuring just 5ft 6, but his build was strong and athletic. Shortly after war broke out, Albert enlisted into the Australian Imperial Force as a low-ranking private solider. He was quickly promoted to acting Lance Corporal and joined the 14th Battalion AIF.
Albert and the rest of the men in his Battalion were sent to the Middle East, where they would undergo training for about two months.

Alberts's first encounter with the enemy couldn't have been any worse. On April 25th, 1915, he was a part of one of the greatest defeats of the war for the Allies, the Battle of Gallipoli. The bloody battle went on for eight months were 8,000 Australians, 3,000 New Zealanders, and 45,000 French and British troops.

Albert and the men of the 14th Battalion were sent to support the ANZACs (Australian and New Zealand Army Corps). They were ordered to defend Courtney's Post from the powerful Ottoman Army, who was relentlessly attacking the men.

In the early hours of May 19th, 1915, the Turkish forces brutally attacked the 14th Battalion, they sent eight bombs into the trench of Albert and his comrades, and three were killed. All other men in the trench were injured except Albert. After the bombing ended, the Turkish forces stormed the trench, and most of the men ran and fled, but not Albert. He stood his ground and maned his gun; he relentlessly fired against the Turkish, so much so that they retreated their assault; Albert stopped the enemy from taking the trench.
Next, Albert and three other men planned a counterattack against the Turkish.

He told the other men to attach bayonets to their rifles. Before the men left to fight the nearby Turkish, Albert said to his men, "I'll go first, follow me", a testament to his bravery and courage.

Shortly after the four men began their assault, one was shot, and Albert asked another brave soldier to help. He asked the new member to provide fire to cover Albert whilst he attempted a flanking maneuver along multiple trenches, crossed the deadly no man's land, and then ambushed the Turkish troops. He shot five men dead and used his bayonet to stab another two.
The Turkish men were so surprised and confused by Alberts's attack that many ran away; Albert even managed to take three Turkish soldiers captive. He went on to hold that trench for the entire night and stopped any enemy troops who tried to take the position.

That wasn't the end of the heroics for Albert. He served again during the Battle of the Somme. Albert had returned from a reconnaissance mission to find the Germans pushing their way through the ANZAC ranks. As he entered his dugout he met two German soldiers who then rolled a bomb in Alberts's direction. The bomb exploded and killed the men alongside Albert.

Not long after the attack, Albert and seven other ANZAC troops headed out of the trench to find over 40 Allied troops being taken prisoner by the Germans. Albert led the charge to liberate them from enemy hands. The Germans fired at the seven men as they ran forward to rescue their military brothers. Then the two groups of men fought hand to hand. Men say that Albert had killed at least 12 men; others say 20. Four of the seven were killed in the fight, and the remaining three were injured, including Albert, who was shot a total of seven times.

Despite serious injuries, the ANZAC troops managed to overcome the Germans and took 50 German prisoners.

Albert was later awarded the Victoria Cross, which is the highest award for bravery available for British and Commonwealth forces; he was the first Australian to be given this award in the First World War. He was also given a gold watch and £500 (which was a lot of money at the time).

The heroic actions of Albert became a legend throughout the Allied forces, the men retold his story countless times, and it helped to boost the morale of the men. The military and the men who served within it were so proud of Albert Jacka that they named a battalion Jacka's Mob.

Jack Cornwall, The boy who never left his Post

John Jack Cornwall was a working-class boy from Essex, England, who became famous after his story was shared by the country; the people rejoiced in his dedication to duty. He was born in 1900 and left school when he was just 13 years old to work as a delivery boy and help earn money for his family. Everyone knew John Jack Cornwall as Jack.
Until July 1915, when he joined the Navy and was trained as a shipboy.

He was well-liked by his commanders and achieved high marks in his gunnery and seamanship training. In the early summer of 1916, Jack set sail on the HMS Chester. They joined the Scapa flow fleet in the Auckney Islands, the most northern point of Britain.

Jack's job on the ship was to be a sight setter for the forward 5.5-inch gun. This is a very important but also dangerous job. He was responsible for relaying orders sent from the gun officer to the crew and adjusting the sight-setting disc; this was the dangerous part of his job because he had to leave the safety of the gun guard where he was completely exposed to enemy fire.

On May 31st, 1916, HMS Chester was sent to investigate gun flashes; 25 miles ahead from the rest of the fleet, the HMS Chester was alone and vulnerable. Unluckily the ship ended up surrounded by four German ships. Even though they were seriously outgunned, the crew of the HMS Chester open-fired on the enemy, but this was of little use. The four German light cruiser ships bombarded HMS Chester; within just 3 minutes most of the ship's guns were out of action, either because they were damaged or because the crews were dead.

The men aboard the ship were in a frenzied panic. Many men were wounded, and it looked as though the battle was lost. All of Jack's crew were dead, and Jack himself was badly injured. Shrapnel had hit him in the legs and the stomach.

Even though Jack was painfully injured, he never abandoned his Post. He stayed by his gun, waiting for more orders for more than 20 minutes.

Luckily the captain of the ship managed to steer the ship away from the fight before they were sunk, but only after they were directly hit 17 times. Jack and the other 70 injured men were taken to hospital in Grimsby for treatment, but sadly on June 2nd, 1916, Jack Cornwall died from his wounds.

Jack was honored in the newspapers by his senior officers. A public funeral was held in London, and the people demanded that Jack be further recognized for his bravery and dedication.

King George V gave Jack the Victoria Cross. This award was given to his mother at Buckingham Palace. September 21st was made Jack Cornwall's day to remember his brave actions.

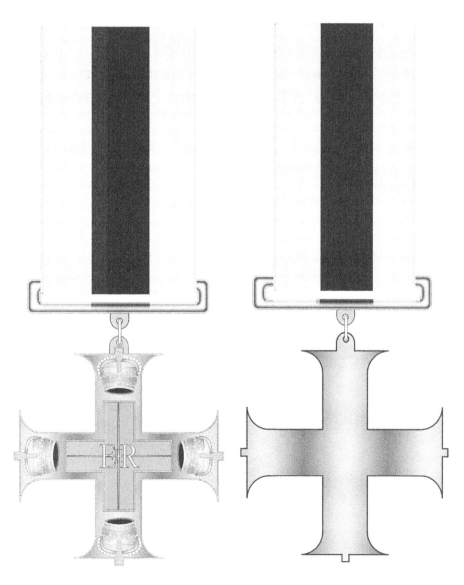

Sergeant Alvin Cullum York

Sergeant Alvin Cullum York was known as Sergeant York, and he went on to be one of the most honored and decorated men in the American Army. He was born in a small log cabin in Tennesse in 1887. He had always been a skilled marksman, which gave him an advantage when he received his draft notice in June of 1917. York never wanted to go to war he was a devoted Christian and believed his religion prevented him from being able to take another man's life, but York was conscripted and had no choice but to join the Army and fight for America.

On October 8th, 1918 York and about 20 of his fellow soldiers were dealing with a group of German prisoners when suddenly they were under attack from a German machine gun. Many men were killed, and York was now the highest-ranking soldier and therefore in charge of the seven remaining men.

York told the men to guard the German prisoners while he single-handedly attacked the machine gun positions. He killed several German soldiers with his rifle but quickly ran out of ammunition; when a group of German soldiers was charging toward him with their bayonets York used his pistol to shoot them all.
By the end of the event, York had killed 20 men, taken 35 machine gun positions, and captured over 100 men.

Army officials didn't believe that York was telling the truth, so the authorities investigated to find out what really happened; their investigation found that York was telling the truth, and he was confirmed as a war hero.

Back in the U.S, York became a celebrity; he was adored by the nation. The Army gave him the medal of honor, and movies were made about him.

After the war, York formed his own Bible school.

400 AMAZING SECOND WORLD WAR FACTS

The nature of war has been constant throughout history, but the methods and mechanisms used to defend and attack change as time passes by; World War II was witness to some extraordinary and world-changing developments in science, engineering, medicine, and mechanics. Let's explore these advancements and all the important events during the Second World War with 400 incredible facts.

In 1939 the German army had almost four million men. The German army included six full Panzer divisions (tanks), 86 infantry divisions, two paratrooper regiments (Fallshirmjager), and four motorized infantry units.

A division includes between 12,000 and 25,000 men.

In 1939 the regular British army included over 200,000 soldiers; this figure includes troops from Burma and India (both of which were British colonies at the time). They also had a further 200,000 men in the territorial army, but in the weeks before the start of the war, the territorial army had doubled in size to over 400,000 men.

The British Empire had more fighting men in the countries of its colonies abroad. In 1939 the Australians had a Volunteer Militia of 80,000 men, but they were only capable of defending Australia; they were not intended to fight abroad.

The U.S army was made up of about 200,000 troops in 1939.

The French army included almost one million regular troops in 1939, but they had a further five million men who had been trained and were ready to fight.

The Soviet (Russian) army included almost two million troops in 1939.

The Soviet army is commonly known as the Red Army.

The full name for the Soviet Union is the Union of Soviet Socialist Republics; this is commonly shortened to the USSR.

The Japanese army is known as the Japanese Imperial Army.

At the start of the Second World War, most of Japan's troops were stationed in China.

Before Japan went to war, they had 17 divisions in their military. This number grew to 41 divisions following the outbreak of war.

The Italian army had about 200,000 soldiers in 1939.

The Chinese army grew rapidly in the years leading up to the Second World War. In July 1937, they had about 30,000 troops, by 1940, this number had increased to over 400,000 troops.

During the Second World War, there were two main groups of countries that went against each other. These groups are known as the Axis and Allies.
The Axis Powers include Germany, Japan, and Italy.

The Allied Powers included France, Canada, China, Australia, Britain, the United States, Poland, Belgium, Holland, and the Soviet Union (the Soviets switched sides from the Axis Powers to the Allied Powers in 1941).

Most of the fighting happened in Europe, but war was waged throughout the world, from Africa to South Asia.

Following the First World War, Germany was in total chaos, they were very poor, and the people were suffering. Unemployment was high, and many people lived in extreme poverty and starvation.

1918 to 1923 were some of Germany's worst years of poverty. Inflation was extremely high; because of this extreme inflation, simple and normally cheap things like a loaf of bread cost billions of German Marks (Marks is the name of German money).

The German people felt humiliated and betrayed by the surrender of the German army and the decisions which followed the First World War. The big fines and loss of land and resources left them living in terrible conditions (these conditions and punishments were set out by the Treaty of Versailles). The people were angry, and after being abandoned by their Kaiser in 1918, they wanted new and strong leadership, not the leaders of the establishment they are used to and have been let down by.

Many Germans believed that they lost the war because of negative powers and influences in Germany and not because of any problem with German soldiers or the German army.

Adolf Hitler served as an infantry soldier in the First World War. He joined the Bavarian Reserve Infantry Regiment as a volunteer in 1914. He worked as a Lance Corporal. A mustard gas attack injured him, and he was left partially blind.

Adolf Hitler was born in Austria in 1889. After the First World War, he moved to Munich.

Hitler, who would go on to be one of the most murderous and dangerous villains of the 20th century, started his political rise in September of 1919. He was working for the German army and instructed to watch and report on a group of far-right political figures known as the German Workers Party, who were meeting in a beer hall in Munich.

This is when Hitler met a man named Dietrich Eckhart. Eckhart was a famous German writer and poet who is seen as being responsible for the rise of Hitler from a poor soldier to the leader of Germany.

Instead of spying on the men as he was instructed by the army, Hitler stopped taking notes and began to talk to the men. He stood on tables and gave exciting and loud speeches. The people who listened to him thought he was great; they silently listened to him as he spoke.

Hitler and the other men all shared extreme views about society. They were all antisemitic. This means they hated Jewish people. Men like Hitler and Eckhart believed that Jews controlled the world and they were responsible for GGermany'sdefeat in the First World War; they wanted revenge against the Jewish people for this.

Eckhart wrote a poem before meeting Hitler. In this poem, he described the future savior of Germany. He wrote that this man would be a brave German soldier, and he would restore Germany to glory. He called this man the Messiah. When Eckhart met Hitler, he believed that Hitler was the man he had predicted would come to save Germany.

Eckhart mentors Hitler helping him to rise politically and fulfill EEckhart'sdream of a powerful and proud Germany. Eckhart even gives Hitler new and respectable clothes to wear to impress the people Eckhart introduces to Hitler.

Hitler becomes the Head of Propaganda for the German Workers Party.
In 1920 the German Workers Party became the National Socialist German Workers Party. Commonly known as the Nazis.

The Nazis used the slogan Germany Awake! They also began using the famous swastika as their emblem.

In 1920 Hitler founded his paramilitary group known as the Sturmabteilung (the SA), which means Assault Division in English. They wore brown uniforms, and the job of the men in this group was to protect the Nazis at gatherings and attack their opposition.

Other names for the SA include Storm Troopers and the Brown Shirts.
Hitler and members of the Nazi party became friends with a German army officer named Captain Ernst Rohm. The captain, who was nicknamed the Machine Gun King, gave the Nazis access to weapons, fighting men, and money.
At the height of German poverty, Hitler and his allies planned an attack on the German government. In November 1923, Hitler and 2,000 of his supporters (from the SA) attempted to take control of Munich. This event is known as the Beer Hall Putsch.

The takeover failed. 16 Nazies and four German officials were killed. Hitler went to prison for treason.

Hitler was loved when he went to prison. The other prisoners treated Hitler as a hero.

During Hitler's time in prison, he wrote his famous book named Mein Kampf (which translates to My Struggle). In this book, he describes his plans for Germany and his hatred for Jewish people.

In his book, Hitler predicts that a European war would lead to the extermination of all Jewish people in Germany.

After a short time in prison, Hitler was released. He then spent his time building up the Nazi Party. Despite his best efforts, he only managed to get 2.6% of the German vote in the election of 1928, which was less than he received in the 1924 election, where he received 6% of the vote.

Life got better for the German people in the mid-1920s. More jobs were available, and inflation went down. It looked as though the hard times were over. Unforcanetly, things got worse again during the worldwide global depression, which began in 1929. The depression was caused by a massive stock market crash.

The hard times caused people to be desperate. This made Hitler's ideas more appealing; Hitler promised change, and the people liked it; in his speeches he spoke of completely changing the system that had caused all their problems. In the 1930 election, the Nazi Party won 18% of the vote. In 1932 they secured 37% of the vote. This marks the time the Nazis became powerful.

Hitler and the Nazis were most popular with the middle class, shopkeepers, and farm workers.

In 1932, Hitler became the chancellor, and the president was Paul Von Hindenburg. Hindenburg and his allies believed they could control Hitler and stop him from doing anything dangerous. This turns out to be one of the biggest mistakes of the century.

In 1931, Ernst Rohm Took over the SA. He grew this small paramilitary group from just a few thousand men to over two million, which was 20 times bigger than the German army.

In February 1933, the Reichstag fire took place. It was set on fire by communists, and Hitler knew he could use this to his advantage. Just days later, Hitler won 44% of the vote. He joined forces with the Nationalist Party; together they had a majority.

Hitler ordered the arrest of all communist leaders in Germany.

At the end of March 1933, the Enabling Act was created. This gave Hitler the power to govern Germany without passing laws through the Reichstag. Hitler was now a dictator and had full control of Germany.

In July 1933, all political parties were outlawed. Only the Nazi Party could exist, and all other political groups were illegal. This marks the end of democracy in 20th-century Germany.

In 1933 the Nazi Party called their regime the Third Reich.

The Pope agreed with the Nazis in 1933. This allowed the Germans to increase their power without any pushback from the Catholic Church as long as the Germans agreed not to attack the Church.

The books of Albert Einstein, Sigmund Freud, H.G Wells, and many others were burned by the Nazis in the early 1930s.

Hitler outlawed trade unions. The leaders were arrested and imprisoned.

Hitler established his own legal courts. The judges were all made to swear an oath to Hitler and the Nazi Party.

The Night of the Long Knives took place in June 1934. Hitler ordered the murder of 400 members of the SA and many of his remaining political opponents, including Ernst Rohm. Hitler did this because Rohm began demanding that Hitler let the SA take over the German army and establish socialism in Germany as Hitler had promised. Hitler knew that this would upset the wealthy businessmen of Germany, and therefore, this was not a good option. The attack was carried out by the SS, who was Hitler's personal bodyguards.

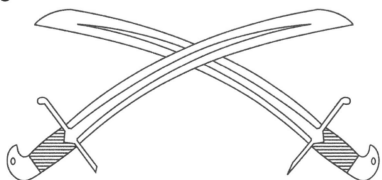

The SS is an abbreviation for Schutzstaffel, which means Protective Echelon in English. The men in this group were described as political soldiers and were some of the most brutal men to serve the Nazi Party.

After the Night of the Long Knives, there was no longer any political opposition against the Nazis; people were too scared to speak up.

In August 1934, the president of Germany, Hindenburg, died, and Hitler became Fuhrer. He also made himself the leader of the German army, and all the soldiers were made to swear an oath to Hitler. At this point, Hitler was the absolute ruler of Germany, and no one could

Hitler wanted to regain the lost territories of Germany and gain new lands to the east. He needed this land because the German people needed what he called living space (Lebensraum) so they could grow their population and expand the Aryan race.

His next step was to begin rearming the German army; this was a violation of the Treaty of Versailles.

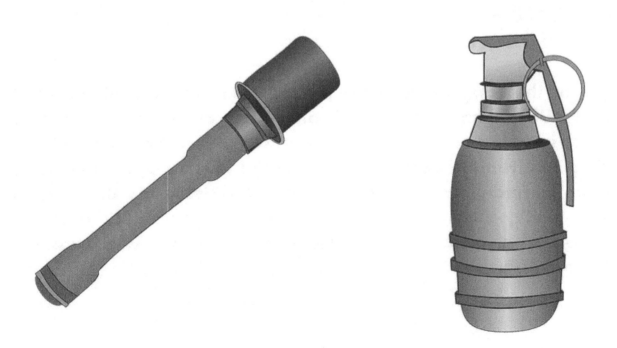

In October 1936 Hitler signed an anti-Soviet alliance with Italy. This was known as the Rome-Berlin Axis.

Shortly after, the Japanese joined this alliance too. The three nations became the Axis Powers and were all anti-communist.

In 1938 Hitler sent troops to neighboring Austria and occupied the nation without resistance from the Austrian military.

In 1939 the Nazis took Czechoslovakia; during this take, over 260,000 Jewish people were killed. Hitler managed to take full control of the two countries without any opposition from foreign powers, but Britain and France had promised military support if they invaded Poland.

In 1939 the leader of the Soviet Union was Joesph Stalin.

The international community was shocked by Hitler and the Soviet Union leader Joesph Stalin when the two leaders signed the German-Soviet Nonaggression Pact. This agreement meant that both nations had agreed not to fight each other.

The German-Soviet Nonaggression Pact made it possible for Hitler to fulfill his promise to the German people and take territories to the east to give them the living space they want without the risk of war with the Soviets to the east.

Germany invaded Poland from the west on September 1st, 1939. World War II had now begun.

The Second World War will go on to be the deadliest war in human history. Over 40 million people died during the long and bloody conflict.

Two days after Germany invaded Poland, Britain and France declared war against the Germans. Britain and France formed the start of the Allied forces; this alliance of countries also included their overseas territories.

Two weeks later, the Soviet Union invaded Poland from the east.

The Polish were able to mobilize about one million men after they were invaded.

The Germans invaded with over 1.5 million troops.

Even though they were able to muster so many men so quickly, they lacked the equipment and technology that the Germans had. The Polish forces had no tanks and very few armored vehicles.

The Polish still had a military force focused on outdated cavalry divisions; horses were no match for German tanks.

They were also outgunned in the sky. The Germans had about ten times more aircraft than the Polish, and German aircraft were of superior quality.

The German army and Luftwaffe (air force) attacked Poland so quickly and aggressively that they were almost wholly beaten before they could even act.

The Luftwaffe destroyed Polish cities with their relentless bombing campaigns, and entire sections of Polish cities were reduced to rubble. The Germans targeted railway stations, roads, and power stations to cause maximum damage.

The invasion started in September, and by October 5th, the majority of the Polish forces were defeated. However, guerilla warfare took place between the remaining Polish Resistance and the Germans until mid-winter.

About 70,000 Polish troops died, and 130,000 were injured during the brief fight.

Casualties for German forces were low; only about 45,000 troops were killed or injured during the Polish assault.

The Nazis took over 700,000 Polish POWs (prisoners of war), although over 10% managed to escape.

The operation name given to the German invasion was Fall Weiss, which is German for Plan White.

The Polish forces fought bravely against the German and Russian forces. Still, by 1940 they were completely overrun by the enemy and the country was divided and occupied by the Soviets and the Germans.

The Soviet Army then went on to invade other surrounding countries, including Estonia, Lithuania, and Latvia.

The USSR took Estonia, Lithuania, and Latvia without war; the Soviets threatened these countries and allowed them to bring Russian soldiers onto their territory without any resistance.

The Soviets gave a similar ultimatum to Finland, but they chose to fight and resist.

Finland had about 200,000 soldiers in its army.

The Soviets brought over one million troops to fight in the Russo-Finish war, which began in November 1939.

The Soviets also had over 1000 tanks.

Finland is a cold country, some parts of which are within the Arctic Circle; because of these cold temperatures, both armies had to use snow sleds to get around the frozen land.

It wasn't easy for the Soviets to invade Finland. The country was heavily fortified. The Mannerheim Line had been built to defend Finland from any Russian invasion, and it protected them for many weeks.

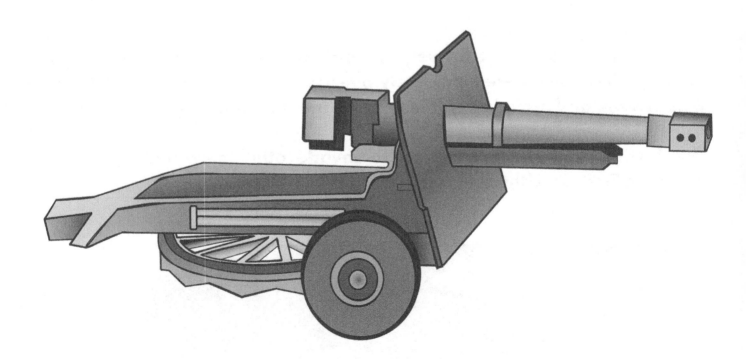

The Mannerheim Line is a defensive system made up of reinforced concrete structures.

After the Mannerheim Line was broken by heavy bombardment from Soviet artillery, the Finnish surrendered to the Soviet Union; their surrender was signed in the Treaty of Moscow.

October 1939 to April 1940 is a period called the Phoney War. It was given this name because, for the six months, very little fighting occurred between the powers.

The Phoney War ended when Germany mobilized troops and invaded neutral Norway. The invasion began on April 9th, 1940.

The Germans quickly took Norway, including its capital city Oslo; despite the Allies sending help and the Norweigan Army fighting to stop the invasion, they were no match for the German army.

Although the Allies were able to recapture areas in Southern Norway, they quickly had to abandon the area when the troops were needed in mainland Europe.

On June 7th, 1940, the Norweigan King Haakon VII, the Norweigan government, and all Allied troops left Norway. The country was now in total control of the Nazis.

During the years of Nazi occupation, the people of Norway resisted the Germans with strikes, sabotage, and protests. This led to martial law and death sentences being used against the people; this never stopped the Norweigan resistance; they continued their work fighting against the German occupation throughout the entire war.

On May 10th, 1940, the Germans invade Belgium; on this very same day, Winston Churchill becomes the leader of Britain.

The Battle of Belgium began in near silence; German paratroopers quietly flew into Belgium using gliders. These men were some of the most elite members of the German forces.

The German paratroopers who were dropped in Belgium destroyed the defenses of a fortress named Eben-Emael.

The next day 1000 Belgian troops who manned the fortress surrendered to the German paratroopers.

On May 13th, 1940, German troops crossed over the river Meuse.
The Germans used Stuka dive bombers to break through the French defenses.

French defenses relied on the Maginot Line, which was made up of fortified pillboxes and other defensive structures, including underground bunkers and minefields.

The Maginot Line was named after its creator Andre Maginot, who was the Minister of War for France from 1929 until 1931.

In today's money, the Maginot Line cost over $9 billion to build.

The Maginot Line was over 280 miles long.

Unexpectedly, the German generals sent the majority of the military through the Ardennes Forest, which the Allies believed would be impassable because of the thick and hilly terrain.

The Germans spent less than six weeks invading Belgium, the Netherlands, Luxembourg, and France.

A key reason for the German army's success in invading countries like France, which were considered to be one of the most powerful military forces in the world, was Blitzkrieg or Lightning War. This type of warfare is very fast. The Germans rapidly moved through the land with heavily armored vehicles, tanks, and infantry troops. They also use air support to bombard the enemy with the force of the Luftwaffe and quickly overcome their opponent's defenses.

The Germans had quickly conquered most of Europe, but strangely on May 24th, 1940, Hitler ordered his troops to stop the invasion.

The unexpected halt of the German invasion was a miracle for the Allied forces, especially the British; it allowed the Allies to evacuate hundreds of thousands of troops through the only remaining seaport, Dunkirk.

On May 26th the British began the evacuation from the beaches of Dunkirk.

The British had to race against time to evacuate as many troops as possible before Hitler lifted the halt order. Damage to the harbor, caused by the Luftwaffe, meant that it was not possible to use large ships to bring the troops to safety. Instead, they had to use small vessels, ferrying the men back across the English Channel in small groups.

The mission to rescue the troops at Dunkirk was called Operation Dynamo.

About 850 privately owned small boats were used in the rescue between May 26th and June 4th.

Some brave civilians sailed across the channel to rescue the stranded men.

Overall, 336,000 Allied troops were saved, which was considerably more than British command had predicted.

Over 200 ships were sunk by the Germans during the evacuation.

On June 10th, Italy declared war against Great Britain and France.

The leader of Italy at the time of the Second World War was Benito Mussolini.

On June 22nd, the French reached an Armistice with the Germans and Italians, this agreement came into effect on June 25th, and the fighting ended with the Nazis and the Allies on mainland Europe.

Following victory in Europe, Hitler's biggest enemy in the west was now Great Britain.

Many historians look at Hitler's halt order as one of his biggest tactical mistakes. If the Germans had carried on, they might have killed or captured most of the BEF (British Expeditionary Forces), and the war may have had a different outcome.

Hitler had wanted to avoid war with Britain and have them as an ally. He once said, "Despite my sincere efforts, it has not been possible to achieve the friendship with England which I believed would have been blessed by both."

The British Foreign Secretary, Lord Halifax, had tried to convince other members of the British government to agree to a peace settlement with Hitler. He believed it would be better to avoid war, but Prime Minister Winston Churchill did not trust Hitler.

Britain and Nazi Germany do not reach a peace deal, and the leader of the German Luftwaffe, Hermann Goring, plans to defeat Britain from the air before the ground army makes the trip across the English Channel and takes Britain.

The Germans had 1,300 bombers, 900 single-engined, and 300 twin-engined aircraft.

The Battle of Britain began on July 10th, 1940, and lasted for over three months until October 1940.

The Battle of Britain is also known as the Air Battle for England.

Goring used the Luftwaffe in different ways to try to destroy the RAF. In July, German aircraft attacked airfields and ports.

During August 1940, the intensity of German bombing raids massively increased. At the peak of the Battle of Britain, the Germans were sending over 1500 aircraft a day to attack Britain.

The RAF only had 749 available aircraft to fight the Germans at the height of the Battle of Britain.

The Germans outnumbered the British pilots, but the Germans were disadvantaged. The British had radar, which alerted them to the location of German planes, so the Germans could not make surprise attacks.

The Germans were disadvantaged because they had to travel many miles to get to Britain; this meant they were limited by their fuel and range, and the British did not have these limitations.

Another cause of British success during the battle is the lack of organization on the part of the Germans. Sometimes they would target ports and shipping, other times, they would bomb cities like London, and sometimes, they aimed for the RAF Fighter Command.

By the end of August, the Germans had lost over 600 aircraft, whereas the British had only lost 260.

The Germans struggled to produce aircraft quickly enough to replace the ones that were being shot down.

The British carried out a counter-attack against the Germans when they bombed the capital city of Germany, Berlin. This made Hitler very angry. He went on to order months of bombings on British cities, especially London.

By the end of the Battle of Britain, the Germans had lost 1,700 aircraft, and the British lost about 900.

The RAF was victorious in the Battle of Britain; the Luftwaffe had failed to quickly defeat the British, which meant it was not possible to invade England.

On April 6th, 1941, Germany invaded Greece and Yugoslavia.

The Germans sent 24 divisions and 1,200 tanks to fight them. The Greeks had 15 divisions, and in Yugoslavia, they had 32 divisions.

Again the Germans used air support and heavy artillery to take territory quickly.

By May 11th, most of Greece was in control of the German forces.

Over 50,000 British troops were evacuated from Greece.

220,000 Greek soldiers were captured and taken as POWs.

Around 20,000 British (or Commonwealth) soldiers were captured.

The Allies and Axis went to war against each other in North Africa.

Egypt and modern-day Libya (in 1940, it was named Cyrenaica) experienced the majority of the fighting.

On December 7th, 1940, in the desert of Egypt, 30,000 British troops battled with 80,000 Italians. The British were led by Major General Richard Nugent O'Connor.

The British were outnumbered, but they still had the advantage because they had more tanks; the Italians had just 120, whilst the British had almost 300.

Three days after the attack had begun, the British had taken over 40,000 Italian troops as prisoners of war.

The Italians retreated to Cyrenaica, where the troops took shelter in a fortress.

The British planned an assault on the fortress, and after three days, the Italians surrendered. The British captured a further 45,000 men.

The British needed to take the port of Benghazi, which was held by the Italians. O'Connor had planned to attack the Italians there until he received intel that they were abandoning the port.

On February 5th O'Connor led his men to intercept the fleeing Italian forces. The British traveled 170 miles in around 33 hours to meet the Italians.

The next day on February 6th, the British and Italians met, and a day of the fighting took place.

3,000 British troops took on over 30,000 Italians and took most of them prisoner.

After success in North Africa, Winston Churchill ordered the number of troops in the area to be massively reduced so that they could be sent to Greece.
The Germans then sent the military to support the defeated Italians.

The newly appointed general Erwin Rommel led the German assault.

By April 11th, 1941, the Germans had reconquered Cyrenaica, and the British retreated to Egypt.

On June 22nd, 1941, Hitler went against his Nonaggression Pact with the USSR and invaded Russia.

The Germans used around 150 divisions to take Russia; this included about three million troops, 3,000 tanks, and 2,500 aircraft.

The Russians managed to establish around 300 divisions following the unexpected invasion.

By the end of July, the Germans had moved over 400 miles across the Soviet Union and were just 200 miles from the Russian capital, Moscow.

The German offensive ended when the worst winter in decades came early in Russia. By October 1941, German troops started getting injured by frostbite because of the extremely low temperatures.

The German command had failed to provide the troops with suitable winter clothing, and this made things even worse for the soldiers. Many died from the cold.

The Russians, on the other hand, were well prepared for the bad weather and had suitable winter clothing.

The Russians had troops from Siberia; these men were used to very cold conditions, which made them fight well during the winter.

The Germans suffered heavy casualties when fighting against the Soviet Union; they lost around 730,000 troops in less than six months.

To make matters worse, for the German assault, they had serious supply problems. The men didn't have enough food, fuel, ammunition, or clothing.

Their situation became so bad that in late November, German field marshall Gerd Von Rusted wanted to retreat, but Hitler had sent orders which forbid them from anything but local and temporary retreats.

In July 1942, the Battle of Stalingrad began.

Many historians consider the Battle of Stalingrad the most important battle of the entire war because it is one of the key moments that the German forces began to lose the war.

Stalingrad was a large and important industrial city situated on the banks of the river Volga. The city had many factories which produced weapons and other important materials.

Another important factor that led Hitler to want to take the city of Stalingrad was its name. The city was named after the leader of the Soviet Union, Joeseph Stalin. Hitler believed it would have a big effect on morale if they captured the city, and it would lead to the overall defeat of the Soviet Union.

Hitler's plan to take over the Soviet Union was code-named Fall Blau (Operation Blue).

Initially, the Germans were successful with their invasion. Until Hitler ordered the German army to split into two groups, one remained on the road to Stalingrad, while the other was sent to the Caucasus in the south. This decision allowed the Red Army to retreat eastward and gave them the advantage.

On July 28th, 1942, Joesph Stalin made an order known as "Not One Step Back", which forbids the army from retreating from Stalingrad. He also banned any civilians from leaving. Stalin did this because he believed the troops would fight harder knowing they were protecting women and children.

By November, the Germans had completely encircled Stalingrad; At one point, the Soviets only occupied a nine-mile long, two-mile-wide strip along the River Volga.

But now winter had come and the Germans were again lacking in supplies of basic equipment like medicine, food, and ammo. Hitler ordered the Luftwaffe to take control of supply, but they were not able to provide all the things the army needed.

On November 19th, the Soviet generals launched a counterattack against the tired German forces. The attack was successful.

In December 1942, Hitler ordered field marshall Erich Von Manstein to rescue General Freiderich Paulus and his men, but Hitler did not allow Paulus to retreat. Instead, he only allowed Manstein and his men to head towards Stalingrad. This decision left Manstein and his men doomed because they did not have enough supplies or power to break through the Soviet defense.

The German troops fighting for Stalingrad were now trapped and they had no hope of achieving a victory. The commanders knew this, but Hitler would not agree to allow them to make a full retreat or surrender, even though the Germans were surrounded by seven Soviet armies.

Knowing the battle was lost, Paulus disobeyed direct orders from Hitler, and he and 22 other generals offered their surrender to the Red Army.

By February 2nd, all of the remaining 91,000 German troops surrendered. They were freezing and starving; thousands of men had already died off the battlefield because of the conditions they were living in.

Of the 91,000 troops that were left, only around 5,000 ever made it home.

The Soviets removed around 250,000 Axis bodies from the battlefield. These dead soldiers were German, Romanian, Italian, and Hungarian.

There were around 800,000 Axis casualties during the Battle of Stalingrad.

40,000 civilians died during the battle.

Over one million Soviet troops died in the Battle of Stalingrad.

By the end of the battle, the city of Stalingrad had been reduced to rubble.

Following victory in Stalingrad, the Soviet army went on to liberate much of Russia and Ukraine.

Deaths on the eastern front total around 30 million.

On December 7th, 1941, Japanese Admiral Nagumo Chuichi sailed his fleet of aircraft carriers towards Hawaii. The Americans only detected their presence when the Japanese were just 275 miles off the coast of Hawaii.

The Admiral ordered around 360 aircraft to attack the U.S naval base at Pearl Harbor.

Throughout the morning of the 7th, the Japanese hit the Americans aggressively and caused major damage to American ships and aircraft.

180 American aircraft were destroyed by the surprise Japanese attack.

Eight battleships, three destroyers, and three cruisers were hit and destroyed, Although the Americans were able to fix some of the vessels and use them again.

Over 2000 U.S servicemen and women were killed during the Pearl Harbor attack.

The Japanese attack against the Americans was successful, but they had made one big mistake. They attacked at a time when the Pacific Fleet's three aircraft carriers were away at sea. These vessels would go on to be an important part of the U.S Navy.

The next day on the 8th, the U.S declared war against Japan.

On December 10th the British battleship the Prince of Wales and the battlecruiser the Repulse were sunk by Japanese aircraft.

The Americans, British, Dutch, and Australians joined together to form an allied command. This military alliance is known as **ABDACOM**.

ABDACOM was responsible for protecting Australia, Java, Sumatra, and Malaya.

On February 8th, the Japanese invaded Singapore; by the 15th, 90,000 British, Indian, and Australian troops had surrendered.

By February 25th, 1942, the Japanese had taken all of the nations ABDACOM was supposed to protect, except Java. ABDACOM was then ended.

On February 27th, the Battle of the Jave Sea took place.

The Japanese were victorious against the Allies, only one of their ships was damaged, whilst the Allies lost a total of five ships.

Next, on February 28th, the Japanese began to take Java; by early March, over 20,000 Allied soldiers had surrendered to the Japanese forces.

On April 19th, the U.S military bombed the capital city of Japan, Tokyo. However, they did not do significant damage.

On May 5th, 1942, the four-day Battle of the Coral Sea began.

Many Japanese and American ships were sunk during the battle. One of the ships sunk was the American aircraft carrier the Lexington.

The battle finally ended with the Japanese retreating following serious damage to one of their largest ships Shokaku. The Japanese lost lots of aircraft too.

Next the Japanese planned to take Midway Island, but the U.S Intelligence Services had deciphered the Japanese message encryption, so the information within Japanese messages gave the U.S forces the advantage in the battle.

The Japanese military brought 11 battleships, 44 destroyers, 15 submarines, and many other vessels and aircraft to conquer Midway Island.

The U.S Navy attacked the Japanese fleet on June 6th, 1942, when they were making their way to Midway Island, still over 500 miles away from their destination.

The U.S forces were outnumbered by the Japanese Navy. The U.S had just three carriers, eight cruisers, and 18 destroyers. Although the U.S did have more submarines, 19 in total, and they had 115 aircraft.

All four of the Japanese aircraft carriers were destroyed and one cruiser. The Japanese retreated following the big loss.

By late October 1942, the war in Egypt had turned in favor of the Allied forces. Commander of the British 8th Army, Bernard Montgomery, led an offensive against the Italian and German forces, which held et-Alamein.

The leader of the German troops in North Africa, field marshall Erwin Rommel had been taken ill and was recovering in Germany.

Combined Axis forces in the area equaled around 80,000 troops.

The Allies had about 230,000 men and over 1,000 tanks.

The Axis troops were poorly supplied with ammo, fuel, and food, because of Allied attacks on German supply ships.

For over weak intense fighting between Allied and Axis troops took place. The Allies lost hundreds of tanks, but the Axis had far less and were running out also.

By early November, Rommel knew he could not withstand the Allied forces any longer. He ordered his men to retreat to Fuka. When Hitler heard about this, he immediately ordered Rommel to halt the retreat and retake et-Alamein.

Once again, Rommel was forced to retreat from the position, and this time they would not return to the battle; the Axis Powers had now lost their grip on North Africa.

The North Africa campaign ended when 250,000 Axis troops surrendered to the Allies.

In the early 1940s, most of Europe was occupied by the Germans; the Allies had to find a way to take back those lands and win the war. On June 6th, 1944, more than 150,000 Allied forces landed on a 50-mile-long stretch of French beaches.

June 6th, 1944, is known as D-Day.

The D in D-Day does not mean anything specific. They called the invasion day D-Day because they did not want the enemy to discover the day it would happen.

It took years of detailed planning between Winston Churchill, Franklin Roosevelt, and all the other Allied leaders and generals to plan D-Day. The plan the Allies created was known as Operation Overlord.

To prepare for the day of the attack, the Americans sent over seven million tons of equipment.

American General George Patton commanded that a fake army be used to trick the Germans. They used to blow-up tanks and trucks to make it appear as though the Allies were planning to attack near Pas-de-Calais, which is the closest point between France and England.

The Allied forces confused the German intelligence agencies with fake radio transmissions and spies.

Hitler knew the Allies would eventually try to invade Europe. Rommel planned a more than 2,000 miles long defensive wall known as the Atlantic Wall. It contained bunks, mines, and other obstacles designed to make it hard for the Allies to land on the beaches and easy for the Germans to repel the invading force.

The Nazis placed over four million mines along the French beaches.

The Allies sectioned the 50 miles of beach into five sections. They were called Omaha, Juno, Utah, Gold, and Sword.

D-Day had been planned for June 5th but bad weather caused British General Dwight Eisenhower to postpone it for one day.

The battle began during the night of bad weather when over 1,000 British aircraft flew over the beach, dropping bombs on German positions.

In the early morning, British, American, and Canadian paratroopers dropped in over enemy lines near beach Utah and Sword. The paratroopers were ordered to destroy bridges to halt any German attempt to send reinforcements during the D-Day landings.

The amphibious landings began at 6.30 in the morning on June 6th. This remains the largest amphibious invasion in military history.

The American troops landed on Utah and Omaha beach. The 4th Division attacked Utah beach, and the 1st Division attacked Omaha beach.

The British forces went to Gold and Sword beach. The 50th Division went to Gold Beach, and the 3rd Division went to Sword beach.

The Canadians sent their 3rd Division to Juno beach.

20,000 American troops landed on the three-mile-long stretch of Utah beach at 6:30 in the morning.

The German 709th, 243rd, and 91st Infantry Divisions were protecting the beach.

By the time the Americans had reached their objective and taken Utah beach, around 300 U.S troops had died.

A further 2,499 U.S airborne troops died.

The other beach American troops were sent to retake was Omaha, and it was by far the most deadly beach of them all. It was protected by the German 352nd Division, with over 6,000 troops.

Omaha was an especially hard beach to take because the Germans had the advantage of the tall sea cliffs.

Around 2,400 U.S troops died during the battle for Omaha beach.

The Omaha operation is remembered by many as a disaster; man died when their tanks sunk in the water instead of floating as they were intended to. Twenty-nine tanks were launched, and only two made it ashore.

Despite all the problems and heavy losses, the U.S troops made good progress as they took German defensive positions one by one.

The Germans lost 1,200 troops during the Omaha landings.

The British began the invasion of Gold beach at 7:25 in the morning.

Gold beach was defended by the 716th Division and parts of the 352nd.

In total, 25,000 British troops landed on Gold beach.

The Allied troops secured the 5 miles stretch of beach and a further 6 miles inland.

400 British soldiers died during the landing on the Gold beach.

The British also invaded Sword beach at 7:25.

A total of 29,000 Allied troops landed on Sword beach, and around 600 died.

The German 716th Division and 21st Panzer Division protected Sword beach.

Out of the 6,000 British Airborne Division, around 1,500 died or were wounded during the D-Day landings.

At 7:55 on the morning of June 6th, 1944, the Canadians landed on Juno beach.

30% of the vessels used to land on beach Juno were destroyed or damaged.

Beach Juno was defended by the German 716th Division.

Out of around 21,000 Canadian troops who landed on Juno beach, 1,200 died.

The D-Day landings were all successful, and this point marks the moment that the Allies began to win the war.

In the weeks following the D-Day landings, the Allied forces took a total of 350 miles of territory.

Following Allied success on the battlefield in northern France, the French Resistance in Paris staged an uprising on August 19th, where the people turned against the occupying German forces.

A French division being led by General Jacques Leclerc received the surrender of the German military forces who held Paris, and on August 25th, the city of Paris was liberated.

Hitler once again ordered the German Army to fight; he forbid any retreat; this was a big mistake on Hitler's part because it prevented the Germans from regrouping in safety and then rejoining the fight.

On September 3rd, Montgomerys 2nd Army took Antwerp in Belgium. This was important because the seaport of Antwerp was still intact and could be used to bring in important supplies for the war effort.

The first German city to be taken by the Allies was Aachen in West Germany.

It took months to take Aachen because it was heavily defended by the German Army, but on October 20th, it finally fell to Allied control.

By the fall, the Allies had 25 aircraft for every one aircraft the Germans had, and the Allies had 20 tanks for every one tank the Germans had.

In October 1944, Hitler had decided to concentrate all his forces on the war in the west. He made a decree that all German men ages 16 to 60 had to join the Volksturrm (the Home Guard), so he could use all his remaining forces to fight on the Western Front.

By the end of 1944, Hitler had increased his reserve of men and now had fresh soldiers ready for battle in large numbers along the front.

To the shock of the Allied Powers, the Germans launched a counteroffensive in mid-December 1944.

The Nazis chose to attack the Allies at their weakest point through a hilly and tree-covered area of the Ardennes, where the Americans were on guard.

The Germans used 24 divisions for their counteroffensive attack in the Ardennes.

This German counter-offensive marks the start of the famous Battle of the Bulge.

The Battle of the Bulge lasted for exactly one month; it started on December 16th, 1944, and ended on January 16th, 1945.

The battle is named the Battle of the Bulge because of the bulge which German forces pushed through the Allies' defenses and lines.

The Germans had the benefit of surprise for their attack, this confused the Allied forces, and the Germans were able to make good ground during the initial hours and days of the counteroffensive.

By the end of December, the German assault slowed down. This was partly due to fuel shortages.

On January 3rd, the U.S First Army began its counteroffensive to push the Germans back.

After much fighting, the Germans tactically withdrew from the Ardennes.

The Allied Powers lost around 75,000 troops, whereas the Germans had more casualties with a total of 120,000.

The Battle of the Bulge would end up being the last major German offensive of the Second World War.

With the pressure on the Germans on the Western Front, the Soviet Union advanced on German territories; in the summer of 1944, they had retaken Russia, Ukraine, and eastern Poland.

In August 1944 the Red Army crossed over the German border and began their advance through the fatherland; they first invaded Germany through East Prussia.

By January 1945, the Soviet troops were only around 100 miles away from the capital city of Germany, Berlin.

The U.S and Japanese Navy engaged in the largest naval battle of history, in October 1944, in the Battle of Leyte Gulf.

During the Battle of Leyte Gulf, the Japanese used kamikaze pilots for the first time.

During the war, around 2,800 Japanese kamikaze pilots died, during which 32 Allied ships were sunk.

In February 1945, U.S Marines landed on the beaches of Iwo Jima, and for the next five weeks, they fought fiercely in battle, which will decide who would control the strategically important island.

1. The island of Iwo Jima was particularly important to the Allies because of the three airstrips on the island and the location of the island, just 750 miles away from Japan, making it a good place to use as a base for an invasion.

The Battle for Iwo Jima is one of the bloodiest fights of all of the Second World War. Of the 21,000 Japanese troops, only about 200 of them survived.

7,000 U.S Marines died in the battle for Iwo Jima.

The famous photo of American troops raising the U.S flag was taken during the Battle for Iwo Jima on Mount Suribachi by photographer Joe Rosenthal. The photo won the Pulitzer Prize.

The U.S declared a victory on the 26th of March, but they continued to find Japanese soldiers in holdouts in the jungle and caves. In fact, some soldiers remained in hiding on the island in 1949, four years after the war had ended.

On all fronts, the Allies are firmly winning the war by 1945, the only question is when will they win?

Just as the end of war is so near, on April 12th, 1945 the Americans suffer the death of their president Franklin Roosevelt. Harry Truman replaces him.

German troops in Italy surrendered on April 29th.

By April 1945 U.S and Soviet troops had met up during their advance through Germany.

Soviet and Polish troops battled to capture the city of Berlin.

On April 30th the Reichstag in Berlin was captured and this represents the final fall of the Nazis.

On the same day that the Reichstag is captured by the Allied forces, Hitler commits suicide in his bunker.

The city of Berlin formerly surrenders on May 2nd, 1945.

The German military in the west of Europe offers their unconditional surrender on May 7th and the remaining German soldiers to the east of Europe surrendered on the 9th.

The British declare May 8th VE Day (Victory in Europe Day), VE Day marks the official end of the war in Europe.

On July 26th the Allied forces issued a declaration to Japan, they call on Japan to surrender or face further attacks.

The Japans never agreed to surrender and on August 6th, 1945 a U.S B-29 dropped the first-ever atomic bomb ever used in the history of warfare on the city of Hiroshima.

The Atom Bomb pulverized everything within a four-mile radius of the drop point and 70,000 people were killed in one moment.

The Japanese leaders did not understand the devastation of the atomic bomb after Hiroshima, so they did not immediately surrender.

A second atomic bomb was dropped on Nagasaki and instantly killed another 40,000 people.

The combination of the dropping of the second atomic bomb in Nagasaki and the declaration of war from the Soviet Union forced the Japanese to surrender. On August 10th, 1945, the Japanese Imperial Army offered their conditional surrender to the Allies, their only condition being that the Emperor remained in power following the surrender. The Allies accepted these terms.

Japan then formalized its surrender to China on September 9th; this marked the final surrender of the Second World War and the end of all fighting.

If Japan had not surrendered, the Allies would have dropped a third nuclear bomb, this time with a target of Tokyo.

One of the main objectives of the Nazis during the Second World War was to exterminate the entire Jewish population. During the Second World War, around six million Jews were killed; the purposeful killing of the Jewish people is called the Holocaust.

Around five million non-Jewish people were killed during the Holocaust too. People who the Nazis considered to be undesirable were killed; these included gypsies, disabled people, and people from nonwhite backgrounds.

About 1.2 million Jewish children were killed during the Holocaust.
Total deaths caused by Nazi concentration camps and the Holocaust were around 12 million.

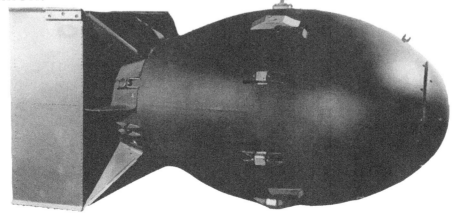

Around five million non-Jewish people were killed during the Holocaust too. People who the Nazis considered to be undesirable were killed; these included gypsies, disabled people, and people from nonwhite backgrounds.

About 1.2 million Jewish children were killed during the Holocaust.

Total deaths caused by Nazi concentration camps and the Holocaust were around 12 million.

Around half of all the Jewish people killed during the Holocaust were from Poland.

The people who the Nazis wanted to kill were first rounded up and put into locked communities called ghettos. They were stripped of all their property and belongings and put on tightly packed cattle trains to be sent to concentration camps.

Jews were also forced to wear yellow stars on their arms. This star is the Star of David and represents Judaism.

The Nazis had considered sending the Jewish people to the island of Madagascar off the coast of Africa.

Concentration camps were used to kill Jewish people, often in gas chambers using poisonous gases. They killed people with gas because it was fast and cheap. The Nazis wanted to kill as many Jewish people as quickly as possible, so they could reach their goal of eliminating all Jewish people in the world.

Jewish and non-Jewish people were also shot. Others died from starvation or exhaustion, as they were made to do manual labor and given very little to eat.

There were a total of six concentration camps created by the Nazis. One of the most notorious German concentration camps is named Auschwitz-Birkenau and it was built in Poland.

1.3 million people were sent to Auschwitz. 1.1million of which were Jewish.

About 85% of all the people who went to Auschwitz were murdered.

Auschwitz was liberated in 1945 by the Soviets. Only 7,000 people remained in the camp; they were all very weak and sick.

Many survivors of concentration camps were so sick that they died shortly after being liberated by the Allies. At Belsen Bergen, a Nazi concentration camp in northern Germany, 13,000 prisoners died after liberation.

A huge pile of over 110,00 pairs of shoes was found at the camp; they also found 12,000 pots and 3,800 suitcases.

The Jewish people faced a terrible life during the war, but some people did try and help them. Including Oscar Schindler, the famous Hollywood movie Schindler's List was made in honor of his efforts to help the Jewish people who worked in his factory.

During World War II women had to take on the roles that men had traditionally done before so many of them went to war. Over 350,000 women served in the U.S military throughout the war.

Women who already had a pilot's license were eligible to join the Women's Airforce Service Pilots (WAPs). They helped to transport aircraft and cargo. By the end of the war, women represented over 65% of the aircraft workforce, whereas, before the war, women only made up about 1% of the workforce. Out of the 1000 women who served in the WAPs, 38 died.

In Britain in 1941, women were called up to join the war effort; they were recruited to work as ambulance drivers, engineers, mechanics, nurses, and fire engine drivers.

Queen Elizabeth II (at the time, she was Princess Elizabeth) served in the Auxillary Territorial Service ATS; she drove ambulances during the war.

Around 80,000 British women joined the Land Army; they had the important job of making sure the British people did not starve. Many had to go to remote and isolated parts of the country to work the land.

Winston Churchill selected 60 women to join the Special Operation Executive SOE. These women parachuted behind enemy lines in Nazi-occupied territory with a mission to create a secret army of resistance fighters to help prepare for the coming D-Day.

One of the most famous women who served in the SOE is Vera Leigh, she was deployed in France and later captured and killed by the Nazis. She was awarded the King's Commendation for her bravery.

Children who lived in British cities, especially London, were evacuated to the countryside to keep them safe during the German bombing raids.

Parents of children eligible for evacuation were given a list of required items. This list included a gas mask, handkerchiefs, soap, a warm coat, and slippers.

Around 1.5 million children were evacuated during the first wave of evacuations.

Some children were sent far away from British shores to Canada, South Africa, and America.

Children helped with the war effort by working as fire spotters and messengers for the Home Front. Others collected scrap metal to be used in war-related production.

Children in America joined the war effort in any way they could. They too, collected scrap metal to be used to produce everything from weapons to machinery. They also used their pocket money to buy war bonds.

Children in both America and Britain could join the Boy Scouts or Girl Guides and help support the war effort through the work the organization does.

In Nazi Germany, it was illegal for children to join the Boy Scouts. Instead, they were expected to join the Hitler Youth. By the time war started over 90% of all German children were involved in Hitler Youth.

By the end of the war, the Nazis desperately needed more troops; they used the boys of the Hitler Youth to fight the Allies.

In January 1940 the British government introduced food rationing, which limited how much food people could buy; this was done to prevent shortages because the food was limited due to Axis attacks on shipping and supplies. Every person was given their own ration book, which had coupons to use in shops.

Sugar, meat, fat, and cheese were all rationed. Other foodstuffs like dried fruit and cereal were rationed depending on availability. Fruit and vegetables were never rationed.

Rations were established in America too. They first rationed tires, but in time rationed items included gasoline, sugar, coffee, meat, fat, cheese and milk. Macaroni Cheese became a popular American dish during the Second World War because it required only a few ration points to buy all the ingredients.

On the battlefield, Allied troops didn't get very good food; in fact, they regularly complained about the quality of their rations. There were two types of rations in the U.S army. The C-Ration and the smaller and more lightweight K-Ration. Soldiers could expect to have biscuits, cheese, meat, beans, instant coffee, sugar, cigarettes, a matchbox, and canned fruit. They also had a toilet roll and a spoon in their ration pack.

Soviet troops had a daily ration of bread, meat, or fish, potatoes, pasta, oil, lard, vegetables, sugar, and tea.

A variety of weapons were used during the Second World War. The M1 Garand rifle was the standard rifle issued to U.S soldiers. It was a semi-automatic weapon and replaced the bolt action rifle used in the First World War. The Commonwealth nations used the Lee-Enfield Rifle.

American factories produced over three million machine guns and seven million riles.

The Mk2 fragmentation grenade was used frot he first time during the Second World War, and it was nicknamed the pineapple grenade because of its knobbly design and shape.

The Germans had the semi-automatic Luger pistol. Allied troops loved to find Luger pistols to take home as war trophies; the German forces got wise to this and booby-trapped them.

The M1 and M1A1 flamethrowers were used by the Allies. They were mostly used to attack fortifications. The flamethrower had a fuel tank with either oil or napalm in the container, which was ignited when a small spark was made. The flame would reach up to 43 meters away.

Destructive machine guns were used widely. The British used the Vickers machine gun, which could fire 450 rounds per minute. The U.S military used the Browning Automatic Rifle BAR, and the Soviets had a gun that could fire 600 rounds per minute.

There were numerous types of artillery pieces used, including, mortars, railroad guns, anti-tank weapons, and howitzers.

The Germans developed the V2 rocket, which was the first of its kind. The V2 was capable of going at 3800 mph and was too fast to be intercepted by air defenses. In September 1944, the Nazis used the V2 rocket to bomb London. There were more than 6,000 casualties.

The Soviets introduced the Katyusha in 1941. A weapon that could fire over 700 rockets in a minute.

The Allies used the M4 Sherman tank throughout the war. The Americans produced over 50,000 of them. It was built by Ford and in production between 1942 and 1945.

German tanks are considered the most effective armored vehicles deployed. They produced Panzers and Tigers and used them when they used the method of a blitzkrieg to invade countries.

British engineer Robert Watson Watt was attempting to develop a death ray to destroy enemy planes. Instead, he created radar, which protected the Allies from surprise Axis attacks.

The most deadly weapon used during World War II is the atomic bomb. This weapon started being developed by the Americans in 1940, in a top-secret operation known as the Manhattan Project. All the top scientists in the country worked together to make a bomb using nuclear fission. To do this, the scientists needed uranium and plutonium. On July 16th, the Americans successfully tested an atomic bomb for the first time. The bomb would go on to be used in Japanese cities Hiroshima and Nagasaki, where thousands of people would instantly lose their lives.

Animals were used less in the Second World War than in the First World War. Horses and mules were still used by both the Allies and the Axis to help transport much-needed equipment.

Dogs were used to help guard positions, these were called watchdogs, and they would bark when someone approached. Other dogs were used as attack dogs and would physically fight with the enemy. Dogs also helped send messages between different groups of soldiers.

Two hundred thousand pigeons were used by the British military; some even had cameras strapped to their chest, which took reconnaissance photos of enemy territory.

In Africa and India, elephants were used in a similar way to horses and mules to transport supplies. A famous group of elephants owned by Gyles Mackeral was used to rescue refugees and soldiers who were struggling to make it through the Chaukan Pass. The elephants reached the people in time to save over 100 lives.

Troops in India and Burma had pet mongooses; these animals would kill any close by snakes and save the men from being bitten. They also warned the men when someone was approaching.

Camels were used throughout northern Africa, in Egypt, Sudan, and Tunisia.

The French had a section of men based in Tunisia named the Free French Camel Corps.

Medicine advanced significantly during the Second World War. For the first time, wounded soldiers could be regularly evacuated by the air, this helped get the injured in the hospital much quicker and saved lives.

In 1928 Alexander Fleming discovered penicillin at St Marys's Hospital, London. Antibiotics were commercially available in the 1930s. The use of antibiotics for battlefield infections saved thousands of wounded soldiers.

Vaccines were used during the Second World War to prevent diseases from typhoid, yellow fever, cholera, and smallpox.

Not all advancements in medicine were good; the famous Nazi, Dr. Joseph Mengele, did thousands of horrible experiments on the people in the concentration camps. Most of his experiments were on Jewish and Romany children. Out of the 3,000 twins he experimented on, only a few hundred survived. Dr. Mengele was known by many as the Angel of Death because of the painful and often deadly genetic experiments he did on his patients.

Hitler's nephew, William Hitler, lived in America, and when war between the U.S and his uncle broke out, he joined the U.S Navy. He also changed his name.

In Britain, a soldier in 1941 would be around $21 a month.

In June 1940, Winston Churchill made his most famous wartime speech when he addressed the House of Commons. He said: "We shall fight on the beaches, we shall fight on the landing grounds, we shall fight in the fields and in the streets, we shall fight in the hills; we shall never surrender, and even if, which I do not for a moment believe, this island or a large part of it were subjugated and starving, then our Empire beyond the seas, armed and guarded by the British fleet, would carry on the struggle, until, in God's good time, the new world, with all its power and might, steps forth to the rescue and the liberation of the old."

During the Blitz in 1940, London was bombed every night for 57 days by the German Luftwaffe. British people hid in bomb shelters and London Underground.

Around 40,000 people were killed during German air raids in Britain.

The Allies carried out bombing raids on Germany from 1940 onwards. Over 600,000 German civilians had died by the end of the war.

In the U.S, the national commissioner for baseball wrote to President Roosevelt and asked if the baseball league should continue during the war. Roosevelt said they should continue to play as it will be good for the morale of America. Most players joined the military and went to war; this meant that other players got a chance to play in the major leagues. Pete Gray had just one arm, but he played as an outfielder for over 50 games during the years of the war.

Japanese soldier Hiroo Onoda came out of the jungle on a Pacific island after 29 years in 1974. He did not know that Japan had surrendered.

The Second World War caused around 60 million deaths and cost an estimated $1 trillion.

Following the war, most people in Europe were unemployed, and many were homeless. Work was hard to find because the bombing raids and supply shortages had crippled all industries.

After the war there were many trials against members of the Nazi regime, they were accused of crimes against humanity and some were punished by death. Many war criminals escaped trial by pretending to be refugees and leaving.

After the war, the U.S and Russia became the dominant world superpowers. In 1947 the U.S and the Soviet Union entered the Cold War, which ended in 1991.

THE STORY OF ANNE FRANK

Anne Frank was born in Germany in 1929; she lived with her Jewish parents and elder sister in her hometown of Frankfurt. By 1933 the Jew-hating Nazi Party had taken over Germany. Jewish people were no longer safe in their communities. Anne's parents didn't think it was safe for her and their sister to stay in Germany anymore and they all moved to Holland.

For a time, Holland was safe, and Anne and her sister lived fairly normal lives, doing things any young girls would. Until June 1940, when the Nazis invaded Holland. Anne and her family tried to escape the Nazis by going to the U.S, but restrictive immigration rules prevented them from boarding a boat.

In 1942 Anne turned 13 years old, and her father Otto gave her a journal as a gift. She began writing down her experiences and feelings as she started her journey through life as a Jewish child in occupied Europe. Just a few weeks after her father Otto gave her the new journal, the family decided to go into hiding with two other Jewish families. They hid inside a hidden attic space above her father's work office. They never left the hidden space of the attic; Anne and he family relied on a small number of family friends to bring them food and other supplies.

Anne regularly wrote about her life hiding in an attic in Amersterdam until one day, in August of 1944, Anne and the others in the attic were discovered by the Gestapo. They were all taken to concentration camps. To begin with, Anne and her family were held in Auschwitz, Poland, but Anne and her sister Margot were later sent to Bergen Belsen in Germany. In 1945 Anne and her sister both died in the concentration camp; their most likely cause of death was typhus.

After the war ended, Anne's father, who was the only surviving person from the attic, was given a collection of papers from one of the people who used to bring them supplies, Miep Gies. Amongst the papers Miep gave Otto was Anne's diary. Her father thought Anne had written beautifully and wanted to share her story with the world. In 1947 her diary was first published in Holland and in 1952, her diary was published in the U.S under the title of Anne Frank: The Diary of a Young Girl.

Anne's diary went on to be an international bestseller, making it one of the most popular books in the world, with over 30 million copies sold. It's even been translated into over 60 different languages.

CALVIN GRAHAM: THE 12-YEAR-OLD NAVY HERO

In the Second World War, every young child growing up in America wanted to help with the war effort. For most, this meant collecting scrap metal, buying war bonds, or making knitted gifts for the men fighting abroad, but for Calvin, this wasn't enough. He dreamed of serving his country and helping to free the world of the terrors of the Axis Powers.

With his ambitions clear and at just 12 years old Calvin asked his friends to fake his mother's signature on his documents and stole a notary's stamp, just so he could fool the military recruitment services. He told his family he was going away to stay with relatives and instead, Calvin made his way to a recruitment screening. He measured just 5ft and 2inches and weighed only 125lbs, but Calvin managed to get selected to join the U.S Navy. In 1942 he was sworn into the navy, and then he was posted as a loader for an antiaircraft gun on the USS South Dakota.

During the Battle of Guadalcanal, the USS South Dakota was hit 47 times by the Japanese Imperial Navy. During the heavy fire, Calvin was blasted down three flights of stairs during an explosion. Young Calvin was injured badly, his face was hit with shrapnel from the blast, but he didn't let this stop him from doing his duty. He helped other injured men aboard the ship; he used belts to stop the bleeding of others and talked to them, trying to keep them calm.

Calvin Graham was an incredibly brave young man who served his country with pride; he was awarded the Bronze Star and a Purple Heart for his courage.

After his mother contacted the navy to tell them of his true age, Calvin was dishonorably discharged and stripped of all his medals and awards and sent to military prison for three months. Because Calvin had been dishonorably discharged, he was refused any disability benefits.

Calvin didn't have an easy life after the war, at 14, he got married and had a child, but by 17 he was divorced. At the same time, he joined the marines, but Graham was hit with disaster again when after three years of service, he fell and broke his back.

After years of unrecognized bravery, President Carter granted him an honorable discharge, but he didn't give him his Purple Heart medal back. Two years after his death in 1994, Calvin Graham's Purple Heart was reinstated and presented to his widow.

THE MOST FEARSOME SOLIDER OF WORLD WAR II: LIEUTENANT-COLONEL "MAD JACK" CHURCHILL

British soldier Jack Churchill gained his notorious reputation whilst fighting throughout the entire Second World War.

Born in 1906, Jack and all his brothers joined the military. After finishing training Jack was commissioned to the Manchester Regiment. He was shortly sent to India, where he went on wild adventures; once he even crashed into a water buffalo.

By the time the Second World War had begun, Jack was no longer in the military. Instead, he had started a career in acting and starred in a movie named The Theif of Bagdhad. Jack's movie career was forced to end quickly when he was called up to fight.

He was especially famous for carrying a longbow and sword into every battle. Jack often said, "Any officer who goes into battle without his sword is improperly dressed".

Jack was an experienced bowman; he had even represented Great Britain in the World Archery Championship in 1939. Jack and his sword and bow were feared by the enemy. One night whilst fighting in Salerno, Italy, he used his sword to take 42 German soldiers prisoner.

As if Jack didn't already have enough things to bring on the battlefield, he also liked to bring the bagpipes and play them on the battlefield. Jack was a great bagpipe player; he had been trained by the Pipe Major of his regiment earlier on in his career.

Jack's heroism didn't end in Italy. In France, Jack and his company of men were trapped, and Jack had been shot in the shoulder. Ignoring his injuries, Jack used his longbow to shoot dead the first approaching German soldier, then he mounted the machine gun and opened fire on the enemy until eventually, Jack had used up all his ammo.

When Jack was in Yugoslavia, he was captured and sent to a concentration camp; at first, the Germans believed that Jack was related to Winston Churchill (he is not), and he was imprisoned with other suspected VIPs. Jack dug a tunnel and escaped the camp; shortly after making his escape, Jack was recaptured and sent to Austria to be held in prison. Jack once again escaped; this time, he got away from the Nazis and crossed over the border into Italy.

Jack Churchill died at 89 years of age at his home in Surrey.

AN AMERICAN HERO: CHARLES CARPENTER

Charles Carpenter signed up to join the U.S Army in 1942, but instead of starting a career as an infantryman, he s sent to fly reconnaissance aircraft. It was his job to scout ahead for the 4th Armoured Division of the U.S 3rd Army in Europe and report back the position of the enemy. For Charles, this wasn't enough. He got fed up with just spotting the enemy; he wanted to fight.

Bold Charles then begins to modify his Grasshopper aircraft. He adds six hand-held rocket launchers, which he straps to the outside of his aircraft. Charles renames his adapted aircraft Rosie the Rocketeer as a tribute to the women in the U.S helping with the war effort. He paints the aircraft's new name on its side. Then in 1944, when the Allied forces were capturing the French seaport of Lorient, he went into battle with his one-of-a-kind aircraft, Rosie the Rocketeer.

Flying the unique aircraft wasn't easy. Charles had to navigate the skies and dodge enemy attacks whilst aiming and firing his bazookas at his targets. To make matters worse for Charles, he only had one shot with each launcher. He had to be incredibly accurate to be effective in battle.

During the months Charles spent attacking the Germans with his airborne bazookas, he managed to destroy at least six enemy tanks, plus other military vehicles. He came close to danger whilst he advanced on the Germans; on one occasion his aircraft was shot in the wing.

His achievements on the battlefield gained him fame back home in America, his photo was in the national newspapers, and everybody loved him. His bravery promoted him to Lieutenant and earned him the nickname Bazooka Charlie.

In 1945 Charles was diagnosed with cancer, and the doctors told him he had less than two years to live. Once again, Charles defied everybody's expectations; after two years, he was still alive and enjoying his life. He raised his daughter, Carol, with his wife. He also went back to his job as a teacher. Charles lived over 20 years following his diagnosis in 1945.

Remember the past

Winston Churchill once said, "Those who fail to learn from history are doomed to repeat it." Churchill's words are as true today as they were all those years ago. That's why the pursuit of historical knowledge is so important.

Made in the USA
Monee, IL
29 October 2022

16715050R00066